800—COCAINE

Mark S. Gold, M.D.

BANTAM BOOKS
TORONTO • NEW YORK • LONDON • SYDNEY • AUCKLAND

800–COCAINE

A Bantam Book / June 1984

2nd printing . . . . . .June 1984   5th printing . . . . . .July 1985
3rd printing . . . . . .June 1984   6th printing . .September 1985
4th printing . . .January 1985

Lyrics from "I Get a Kick Out of You" by Cole Porter © 1934 (renewed) Warner Bros. Inc. All rights reserved. Used by permission.
Lyrics from "Cocaine" by J.J. Cale © 1975 Audigram Music. Used by permission.

Text photographs by Peter Benson, Flat Iron Photographics, Guilford, CT. Courtesy of Fair Oaks Hospital.

Library of Congress Cataloging in Publication Data

Gold, Mark S.
  800–Cocaine.

  1. Cocaine habit. 2. Cocaine habit—United States.
I. Title. II. Title: Eight hundred—Cocaine.
RC568.C6G65 1984   613.8'3   83-45994
ISBN 0-553-34094-8 (lg. paper)

Published simultaneously in the United States and Canada

PRINTED IN THE UNITED STATES OF AMERICA

S   16 15 14 13 12 11 10 9 8 7

With pleasure and humility I dedicate this book to Herbert D. Kleber, M.D., and Robert Byck, M.D., Professors of Psychiatry and Pharmacology at the Yale University School of Medicine. They taught me about cocaine abuse, encouraged my research interests, and armed me with the knowledge and know-how essential to undertaking the 800-Cocaine enterprise.

My brother, H. Scott Gold, J.D., LL.M., spent many daytime, evening and weekend hours researching the cocaine statutes of all 50 states. He shared with me his legal expertise and guided me through the immensely complex issues involved in trying to make the law impact positively and humanely on drug abuse in our society.

Acknowledgments

Lynn C. Landman brought to this work distinguished skills as a writer and editor. Her talent, sensitivity, and inquiring mind have helped illuminate significant medical and social problems. I thank her for her contribution.

A. Carter Pottash, M.D., a brilliant physician, case historian, medical writer and critic helped me to organize my thinking about the nature of drug abuse in general and cocaine abuse in particular. I thank him for his friendship and wise counsel.

Acknowledgments

Contents

Preface

This book is for the many Americans who are curious about, tempted by, and uninformed or misinformed about the nature of cocaine and the consequences of its use. More than 1,350,000 men and women have called 800–Cocaine seeking information and/or help in the first two years since the hotline went into service. This book is a distillation of the answers and the assistance we have provided, and of what we have learned from our callers.

Readers will find information on the nature of the drug; how, when, and where it was discovered; where it is grown; how it is processed and used; how it works; the history of its use, and the dimension of the cocaine epidemic in the United States. They will also find a profile of the "typical" user and what happens to him or her when and if coke use escalates. The side effects of cocaine are detailed, as are the various types of treatment used to free the abuser from the drug. How all of us can participate in stemming the cocaine epidemic is also spelled out.

Answers are provided to the most commonly asked questions. For example, a parent, worried that a child might be using cocaine, could turn to Chapter 3 (question 6) to find out what changes in behavior and personality are typical of the beginning user. Anyone who wants to know the possible dangers associated with coke use should take a look at Chapter 5. For those curious about how to recognize addiction, the test in Chapter 7 will be helpful. The kinds of treatment available, and where to turn for help, are spelled out in Chapters 6 and 8.

The reader will discover that certain ideas are repeated throughout this book. This is deliberate. It is done to emphasize what I consider the key issues concerning cocaine: That it should not be regarded as a benign recreational drug. That its use can exact a terrible toll. That it can cause addiction. That there is no "cure" for cocaine addiction except permanent and total abstention from its use. That it is better to say a firm NO to the drug than to have to deal with its destructiveness once it takes hold.

As a physician, I am committed to the view that the patient is entitled to know all there is to know about any drug or proposed treatment. This book is my way of sharing my knowledge of cocaine's ability to produce euphoria, energy, confidence, well-being, and a special disease we call drug addiction.

—Mark S. Gold, M.D.

1
Everything You Want to Know About Cocaine

An incredible 25 million Americans—one out of every 10—report that they have used cocaine at least once. And every day, some 3,000 teenagers and adults try it for the first time. As many as one million Americans are so dependent upon the drug that they cannot stop using it no matter how destructive it is to their health, to their family life and to their careers. In the first three-month period, 100,000 men and women called 800–Cocaine, the first nationwide cocaine hotline, to ask all sorts of questions about the drug, from whether coke is "really" addictive to where they, a family member, or a friend could get help with a coke problem. For nearly two and one half years the phone continues to ring nearly 1,500 times a day.

What these statistics make clear is that cocaine is no longer uniquely the drug of the very rich, of rock and TV stars, of million-dollar-a-year athletes. Despite its price, which is very high indeed, it is increasingly the drug of middle-class America—of those who still have plenty of disposable income. Among their numbers are doctors, airline pilots, highly skilled factory workers, lawyers, engineers, stockbrokers, computer whizzes, and entrepreneurs. Most of them white, in their 20s and 30s, men and women who are on their way up and who, by most yardsticks used to measure success, are successful.

Most of them first encounter cocaine in a social situation, for instance at a party among friends, or at the office where a fellow worker assures them that a whiff or snort of coke will set them up for that critical meeting with the boss or client. So they try it that first time. For some, that initial snort will be the last. As a 31-year-old advertising copywriter told me, "It was just no big deal. Why waste money and take risks?" For some, it will become a once-a-month treat, like having an occasional gourmet meal in a fancy restaurant. For others, however, their first experience will be followed by a second, a third, and on and on until using the drug in increasing quantity and frequency becomes the most important and driving force in life. Until, in short, they become addicted. Scientifically, there is no way to predict who in a group using the drug for the first time will ultimately become hooked.

This is what happened to John R., a 32-year-old lawyer from the Midwest who checked himself into a psychiatric hospital because cocaine had taken over his life in the four years since he had first used it. His wife was threatening to leave him. He was neglecting his law practice, borrowing large sums of money to support his $3,000-a-week habit, and even stole from his firm when he couldn't get money any other way. He had become totally alienated from his mother, brother and sister, and old friends. He said that he had tried several times over the years to quit, but couldn't. Now he was deeply depressed, was feeling physically ill, and had come to the end of the road.

Nothing in his history could have predicted this turn in his life. His parents loved and admired him, enjoyed his successes as a student and athlete; a brother and sister were companionable and not troublingly competitive. He was exceptionally close to his father, a successful businessman, who had died of lung cancer four years earlier. A couple of paternal uncles were alcoholics, but this was not a problem in the immediate family. John had many friends as well as a good education. While he had recently married a woman his mother disapproved of, his coke problem began long before his marriage.

He had experimented with some drugs in college—marijuana, alcohol, amphetamines (to stay awake for exams)—but not to the point where they ever disrupted his life. He tried coke initially because, he said, it was the thing to do. Its high gave him the extra energy he needed when working long hours to build his law practice. He moved rapidly from occasional, to daily, to round-the-clock use.

He tried several times to cut down, but couldn't. Then he went to a psychotherapist for a while, but at his therapist's suggestion entered the hospital. Although he stayed in the hospital during the difficult period of detoxification and agreed to work on his problem in an outpatient cocaine-anonymous group, John's future prognosis is still extremely guarded. Experience shows that, as with alcoholics, complete and permanent abstention are essential to recovery. And this is a tough challenge to meet, especially since the high that John felt while using the drug was vivid and powerfully attractive.

The High & Crash

Descriptions of cocaine's effects are strikingly similar, whether they come from Freud, an early experimenter with it, or from rock songwriters, cocaine's contemporary troubadors. In general, within a few minutes of taking it, the user is enveloped by a sense of well-being, feels self-confident and strong, exhilarated and capable of taking on any challenge. The drug banishes fatigue and hunger, and reportedly increases sexual interest and performance. These effects last 15–30 minutes—at a monetary cost of approximately $3 per minute.

Some men and women—and their number is growing—become so enamored of the initial high that reexperiencing it becomes obsessive. Frequency and dosage escalate. When such a user comes down off the drug, when he "crashes," the euphoria is replaced by fatigue, depression, irritability, and sometimes by psychotic reactions. Food, hunger, sex can no longer compete with the attraction or importance of cocaine. To such a user, the solution is more cocaine, and the cycle of abuse is under way. There is now evidence that the road from so-called recreational use to abuse may be a very short one indeed.

Given the nature of the drug and how it is believed to work, this is not surprising. Cocaine is a naturally occurring stimulant, an alkaloid, extracted from the leaf of the coca bush. While it is new to most of us, documented use of the coca leaf among Latin American Indians goes back many centuries. In fact, the Incas believed coca to be of divine origin, and it played a central role in their religious ceremonies. It was so highly prized that its use was restricted to the nobility.

Some 400 years ago, the conquistadores observed in what is now Peru and Bolivia that the Indians regularly chewed or sucked wads of moistened coca leaves that had been smeared with ashes in order to extract the cocaine from the leaves. This practice, one observer of the period wrote, "satisfies the hungry, gives new strength to the weary and exhausted, and makes the unhappy forget their sorrows."

These effects have since been corroborated by observation of the Indians who live today in the same geographic area. Poverty-stricken, and working long hours at high altitudes, they too use the coca leaf in the same fashion. Chemical analysis of the leaf shows it to be rich in vitamins, particularly in vitamin C, in thiamine and in riboflavin. The consumption of about two ounces of coca leaves a day provides the Indians with much of their daily vitamin requirement. But it should also be noted that coca and cocaine are not synonymous, and the latter is just one component of the leaf. In addition, there appears to be some evidence that cocaine in the form used today appears to deplete some of the body's store of essential neurochemicals and vitamins. But more of that later.

Cocaine for street use is extracted from the leaf in two relatively simple steps. First, the leaves are placed in a press or steel drum along with sulfuric acid and are crushed into a·mash called pasta, cocaine sulfate. The pasta is then further processed by the addition of a solvent, hydrochloric acid, to eliminate other chemicals. The result is cocaine hydrochloride, which is sold in crystal form or chopped into the white, odorless powder that becomes the active product sold illicitly for so-called recreational use.

To increase their profits, cocaine dealers multiply the quantity of the drug by adding a variety of adulterants of which the user is generally unaware. He or she is paying a high price, $75–$100 a gram, for a product that may consist of 30 percent cocaine and 70 percent various inactive sugars, local anesthetics, or even heroin or other addictive drugs. These adulterants may cause physical problems quite apart from the effects of the cocaine itself. Occasionally, when pure cocaine is used (again unknown to the purchaser) in the same quantity as the adulterated product, it has even greater ill effects and sometimes quickly leads to death.

Cocaine is taken by various routes, and it enters the bloodstream and the brain rapidly from mucous membranes throughout the body. It can be, but seldom is anymore, taken as a drink; it can be applied to mucous membranes of the mouth—including the gums—of genitals or rectum, but this is not common practice either. Most frequently, it is sniffed or snorted through a straw or a rolled up dollar bill—sometimes even a $100 bill. Or a solution of the drug may be injected into a vein. In a somewhat different form, it may also be smoked. Since freebasing, as this is known, is a growing and dangerous new fad, a few explanatory words are appropriate.

For freebasing, ordinary street cocaine is separated from its adulterants by mixing it with water and ammonium hydroxide. The cocaine base is then separated from the water using a fast-drying solvent such as ether. The base is then smoked in a specially-designed water pipe that has a bowl fitted with several layers of stainless steel screens. The freebase is placed on the top screen, is melted to an oil, and is then heated slowly while air is drawn through the stem into the mouth. The cocaine moves quickly, more quickly than by any other route, from the blood-vessel rich lungs to the brain, causing an intense swift rush of pleasure. As Richard Pryor found out, freebasing is distinctly dangerous to the health, quite apart from the problems induced by the drug. Because ether is so highly flammable, it caught fire while Pryor was trying to speed up the drying process and enveloped him in flames in a matter of seconds.

The speed with which the cocaine user achieves his high depends to a great extent on how he administers the drug. It may take three minutes when the drug is snorted, one-half minute when it is injected, and a few seconds when it is smoked.

How cocaine achieves its effect is still a mystery. We have been making progress in understanding how it fools the brain into thinking it is something more important than food, water, sex or survival. It is known that when cocaine or other stimulants (amphetamines, for example) enter the body, they move rapidly from the bloodstream to their target, the central nervous system. At first, cocaine augments the action of the naturally occurring chemicals, the neurotransmitters, that carry messages to the various reward or pleasure centers of the brain. Somehow, the brain is manipulated to provide the sought-after pleasurable sensations until the neurotransmitters are too diminished in numbers to react to the cocaine.

How much of the drug is required to achieve its effects is difficult to say since it depends somewhat upon its purity, whether the user has developed a tolerance to it (requiring increasingly larger doses to achieve the same results), the user's state of physical and mental health, and many other factors. Generally, a "line" of cocaine used for snorting contains about 25–30 milligrams. Called a line because the snorter literally sets up the white powder on a mirror or other shiny surface in a straight line measuring about ⅛th of an inch wide by one inch long, a Beverly Hills host I was told about often provides a gram of coke for his guests (some provide even more), distributed into about 35 lines. About the same quantity, 25–30 milligrams, is used for injecting the drug; less is used in freebasing because the purified form has a greater kick.

What is most important, however, is that many who start by using moderate amounts once in a while escalate their doses, begin to binge, and move swiftly to the most dangerous route by far—freebasing.

By whatever route they use it, Americans consume virtually all of the estimated 50 metric tons (110,000 pounds) of cocaine believed to enter the country illegally ever year, mainly from Colombia, Bolivia, Brazil and Peru. Americans pay as much as $39 billion for it, most of which ends up in the unnumbered bank accounts of the Latin American drug lords who dominate the trade. In Colombia, cocaine exceeds coffee as the country's main export and foreign exchange earner.

The drug lords' tentacles envelop every aspect of the cocaine business. Often, they own the land and dictate the crop that the bone-poor tenant farmers, the campesinos, grow; they own the fleets of planes and boats that carry some of their cargo into the United States; in a very real sense, they own the regiments of runners who literally carry it into the U.S. and connect with their wholesalers, some of them Latins, some Americans, who are the next level in the distribution network. These wholesalers then distribute smaller quantities to local dealers who can be found in virtually ever city in the nation; from them, the drug is sold largely through users, the men and women with whose lives this book is concerned. For as they become dependent on the drug, their income soon is inadequate to pay for their supplies. They become dealers in part to support their own habit. Mind you, these people may be your friends, colleagues, lovers, children—people never before involved in any criminal activity.

The power of the drug cartel to corrupt both their own governments and others' has been documented almost daily, but in my view, the real victims of the cocaine epidemic, in addition to the users, are the American people. We are all victimized in the work place when productivity and efficiency decline as a consequence of coke use. We all pay higher premiums for health insurance because of increasing utilization of physician and hospital services by abusers. A wide spectrum of medical specialists is involved in the care and treatment of cocaine addicts: cardiologists when arrhythmias occur; otolarynogologists when nasal and throat abnormalities develop; psychiatrists to treat hallucinations and depressions; neurologists for the seizure prone; endocrinologists, urologists, and gynecologists to treat sexual dysfunction, to name just a few.

Further, judging from the reports of the effects of cocaine use on family life, its sharp reduction or elimination would unquestionably have a positive impact on the stability of families. It would also reduce automobile accident rates and deaths, since there is mounting evidence that coke and alcohol used together are a lethal combination on the road. Violent crime, felonies, police corruption, overcrowded court calendars, and jails would all be affected were coke to cease to be the drug of choice of so many millions.

2
Profile of the Cocaine User

The phones keep ringing in the 12-foot windowless room. Six people are taking the calls. From time to time, I'm one of them. "Hello, yes this is 800–Cocaine. No, this phone is not being tapped. No, there are no FBI agents or police listening in. No, there are no agents on the premises. Yes, this is private, confidential." Sometimes the caller thanks me, hangs up to weigh whether he believes me. Sometimes the caller, reassured, tells the story:

• A mother in Virginia is desperate because her 21-year-old son, who has always been a model child and student, has stolen $4,000 from the family business in just six weeks. His nose bleeds all the time. He keeps packing it with gauze. He doesn't eat, can't sleep. He finally told her he's on cocaine, is frightened, but can't stop using it. The mother, weeping, asks what she should do. Is he addicted? Is there someplace nearby where he can be taken for help?

• A high school vocational counselor in Los Angeles knows she's in trouble. "My coke habit is so bad I've been buying it from my students. Please, I need a referral to an inpatient program to save my life and career."

• "The last few times I freebased, I had seizures. Does coke *really* cause seizures? If I use less of it, will I be okay? I just won't stop." This from a 31-year-old insurance executive in Connecticut.

• "My friends told me cocaine is not addicting. If it's not, how come I can't stop?"

• This from a 36-year-old bus driver from Chicago. "I spent all of the money my wife and I put aside for Christmas on cocaine. Now I'm crying, depressed, and really believe I should be shot."

Close to 1,250,000 calls have flooded 800–Cocaine, this nation's and perhaps the world's first national cocaine hotline, since we launched it on May 6, 1983. In effect, we invited anyone who wanted to, cocaine user or not, to call us at our expanse to discuss anything having to do with the drug. We were prepared to refer callers to a network of doctors, clinics, and hospitals situated in all 50 states for counseling or medical care. To date, 700 such resources have made themselves available, and their names, addresses, and phone numbers are on our computer to be called up in an instant.

We had a twofold objective in setting up the hotline. The first was to try to be of some help to the thousands and thousands of people out there who, we suspected, needed information on the drug and its effects, and assistance. The second was to fill large gaps in our own knowledge. Until very recently, doctors as well as the general public knew relatively little about the cocaine user/abuser, and what we did know came from limited case reports and laboratory experience published in professional journals, or from sensational stories in the popular media.

We reasoned that our dedicated staff and computerized referral network would help meet our first objective. As to the second, we had a research questionnaire for callers to respond to if they were willing to do so. As a glance at it will show, our questionnaire* was intended to find out who the users are, what kind of work they do, how much they earn, how much they spend on cocaine, how they use it, and what problems they are encountering that compelled them to dial 800–Cocaine.

Five hundred cocaine users, chosen at random from among the first 100,000 persons who called the hotline, agreed to take part in the 20- to 30-minute structured interviews. (All other callers were asked to respond to a shorter version of the questionnaire). Initial recreational use in the group of 500 rather quickly escalated to compulsive use. Men and women who had never in their lives stolen a penny became thieves to support their habit. Previously healthy young people were suffering a variety of physical and mental illnesses as a result of their cocaine use.

*See Appendix A page 74

Profile of the 500

A close-up of the 500 shows that they were about 30 years old, with a majority aged 25 to 40, at the time of their call to the hotline. Some were as young as 18 and as old as 78. They had begun to use coke just under five years earlier. Contrary to popular belief, cocaine abuse is not strictly a male phenomenon. One out of three of the coke users was a woman. The overwhelming majority—85 percent—was white; the rest were Black or Hispanic. They were well educated, on average having completed just over 14 years of schooling. Within the group there were college graduates, men and women with M.D. and legal degrees, business people, educators, engineering Ph.D.'s, and airline pilots with years of training to qualify them for their jobs.

Given this background, it is hardly surprising that these callers were, on the whole, among the top earners in the country. They averaged about $25,000 a year, and of all those who gave their income, an astonishing one in almost seven earned $50,000 a year or more.

Of the 500 respondents, almost two thirds were living in New York, New Jersey, California, and Florida, the rest in 33 other states.

Their Cocaine Use

As noted, they had begun their use 4.9 years earlier, and more than nine in ten started with snorting. At the time of their call, 306 of the 500 were taking the drug intranasally, 103 were freebasing, and 91 were injecting it. The usual history is to start by snorting; then users move either to injecting or to freebasing. About half of the sample were using cocaine daily, at a street cost of $75 to $125 per gram. On average, they were using about six grams a week. They said that they had spent an average of $637 for cocaine in the week before they called the hotline, with a range from about $100 to $3,200. Despite their own reports that they were suffering from a variety of health problems because of cocaine use, well over half said that the major factor limiting their use was the cost of the drug. Fewer than one in ten said a physical or mental problem had ever caused them to stop using the drug. And more than nine in ten said that they had sometimes used their supply of the drug continuously until it was exhausted, no matter how much they had on hand.

Despite the numerous adverse effects of the drug, these survey respondents said that they continue to use it because of its positive effects on their functioning. For example, 82 percent enjoyed the unusual feeling of total pleasantness, the high, that it induced in them; 48 percent said that the drug increased their energy levels and self-confidence; 21 percent said that it stimulated their sexuality. Another 57 percent used cocaine to relieve the boredom of their lives.

However, 80 percent said that when the high wore off, they felt depressed, lost their energy and motivation, and "crashed." Therefore, almost 70 percent reported that they used alcohol, heroin, or other narcotics to relieve or ward off these symptoms when the cocaine-induced euphoria dissipated.

In our questionnaire, we listed 21 physical side effects and 20 psychological side effects that are widely reported to occur when cocaine is abused. We used our own observations and those of other specialists in cocaine abuse to draw up the list. The hotline counselors asked the 500 callers who had agreed to participate in the survey to indicate which, if any, they had experienced.

Their replies provide clear and convincing evidence of the power of the drug to dominate its users even in the face of powerful negative effects. Overall, the respondents reported having suffered an average of 11 of a possible 21 physical side effects, 12 of a possible 20 psychological side effects, and 6 of a possible 14 social and other problems. (All the side effects are shown on the questionnaire.) The five leading physical side effects were chronic insomnia, reported by 82 percent, chronic fatigue, by 76 percent, severe headaches, by 60 percent, nasal problems, by 58 percent, and poor or decreased sexual performance, by 55 percent. Among other serious physical problems reported were seizures and loss of consciousness that, together, were experienced by 26 percent, and nausea and vomiting, by 39 percent.

The leading psychological problems were depression, anxiety, and irritability, each of which was reported by more than 80 percent of the sample. Paranoia, loss of interest in nondrug-related activities, and difficulties in concentrating were each reported by 65 percent or more, while 63 percent reported loss of interest in friends. (Fifty-four percent said that they usually used the drug when they were alone.) Oddly, although increased sexual arousal was given as a reason for continued use of the drug, more than half the sample, 53 percent, noted loss of sex drive. A frightening 38 percent said that they had thought about committing suicide, while nine percent had actually made a suicide attempt.

Random interview surveys conducted in 1983, 1984 and 1985 have allowed us to see the cocaine epidemic evolve. Now the typical user is just as likely to be in St. Louis, Jackson, Houston or Denver as New York, San Francisco, Miami or Tampa. Cocaine is a national problem affecting more and more women, children and people in college. Wealthy users deal and distribute cocaine, steal from work and others as frequently as average income users but they have more traffic accidents (21% rich vs 6%) and more brain seizures (19% vs 11%). With increased disposable income or more cocaine access comes more medical emergencies and addiction.

Dependence, Social Functioning

Another series of items, 23 in all, probed the issue of drug dependence. Typically, the respondents said that 15 of the items described their experience with the drug. Overall, 61 percent believed that they were addicted. Eighty-three percent said that they could not turn down the drug when it was available, and 73 percent, that they had lost control and could not limit cocaine use. Just over half, 52 percent, said that they felt "significant distress" without cocaine, while 80 percent said that if they stopped using the drug, they became depressed or felt other symptoms of the coke crash or lost energy and motivation—all of which describe withdrawal. More than 70 percent reported that they had binged on the drug, that is, that they had used it continuously for 24 hours or more. Sixty-seven percent said that they were unable to stop using it for as long as one month. For 71 percent of the 500 respondents cocaine was more important than food; for 50 percent it won out over sex; for 72 percent it was more important than family activities, and for 64 percent it displaced friends.

Not surprisingly, cocaine abuse led to numerous and serious personal and social problems. For example, 45 percent of the 500 respondents said that they had stolen money from their employers and from family or friends to support their cocaine habit. Fifty-six percent had used up at least 50 percent of their savings; half were in debt, and 42 percent had wiped out all their monetary assets. Thirty-eight and 28 percent, respectively, said they had dealt in drugs or had participated in other illegal activities to obtain the drug. Just under 40 percent had experienced job or career problems, and 17 percent had actually lost their jobs as a result of cocaine abuse. In addition, 26 percent of the 500 had been divorced or had lost a lover because of the cocaine problem, and another 28 percent were being threatened with separation or divorce.

Sixty of the 500 callers, or 12 percent, said that they have been arrested for dealing in or for possession of cocaine; 11 percent have been involved in traffic accidents, and 13 percent were in traffic violations while under its influence.

It is generally believed that people who use the drug by snorting it do not suffer serious side effects. The information from these 500 users does not support this view. They, too, experienced many of the serious physical, psychological, and social problems. However, intravenous users and freebase smokers were the most disabled groups and were more likely to report nearly all of the serious ill effects.

When looked at separately, the experience of the women on cocaine was much like that of the men. They, too, were well educated, earned relatively high incomes, had used the drug for an average of four years, had binged, and reported suffering the same problems as men. A similar proportion had tried to commit suicide. We conclude, as have others, that as women become better educated, suffer the same stresses as men in connection with their careers, earn substantial salaries, and live similar lifestyles, they, too, seek "to be with it," to be part of the crowd, to do what's trendy. Often, this means abusing the same substances—alcohol, cigarettes, or drugs—with the same sorry results.

What we have, then, is a portrait of a very sick part of middle-class America. These men and women are, or have been, your friends, your neighbors, your clean-cut achieving children, husbands, wives, lovers—but coke has caused many to become white-collar criminals. The coke abusers feel themselves to be ill, attribute their illness to coke, and yet are unable and unwilling to try to get the monkey off their backs. While many deny that they are addicts, their descriptions of themselves is the classic profile of the addict. Their lives are out of control.

A 26-year-old nurse is terrified that she will never again get a job in her field because she was caught stealing from her hospital's supply of pure cocaine reserved for anesthesia. A $100,000-a-year garment industry executive, bored and lonely and dissatisfied with his stressful life, despite his business success and a wife and child he cared deeply about, lost it all to his coke habit. A gifted young woman whose talent was discovered when she was still a teenager binged on coke so continuously that she destroyed her looks, her voice, her ability to act, and acquired a chronic illness for which there is no cure.

For all these people, the description of cocaine as a "recreational" or "social" drug is a sick joke. Recreation does not usually take over one's entire life and destroy it. The loneliness of the cocaine abuser makes the view that coke is a social drug a lie. By their own account, use of the drug has cut them off, set them adrift from most of their previously meaningful relationships.

The bottom line is that for many people, perhaps most, there is no really safe way to use cocaine. Use fuels further use. The best and safest response to offers of a snort, even from best friends, and even at the risk of being considered a party pooper, is a firm, "Thanks, but no thanks."

If you find yourself wavering, call 800–Cocaine and ask to speak to a recovering addict. You will find out what it is like to develop a lifelong disability, and you will be able to weigh whether the benefits of cocaine use are worth the risks.

3
Q and A About Cocaine

Judging from the number of questions I am constantly asked about cocaine—from callers to the hotline, from TV talk show hosts, from doctors at professional meetings, from reporters, from friends at dinner parties—people are eager to know everything there is to know about the drug. Here are 24 of the most common questions along with my answers and/or comments. My answers are based on my clinical experience as a doctor working with cocaine-dependent patients, on my training as a psychopharmacologist, the specialty concerned with how drugs and medications act on the brain and change thinking and behavior, on my knowledge of the extensive medical, historical, and professional literature having to do with cocaine, and on my experience and the 800–Cocaine staff's experience in talking with approximately 350,000 cocaine users. Among the leading questions are the following:

1. What is cocaine?
Cocaine is one of the alkaloids extracted from the leaves of the coca plant, which grows largely in Peru and Bolivia but is also cultivated in Central America, Indonesia, and Ceylon, among other places. It is recognized as a stimulant and euphoriant; it achieves these effects by interacting with substances in the central nervous system that carry messages to various parts of the brain. It is a topical anesthetic that blocks nerve conduction of pain. And it is also a vasoconstrictor; that is, it narrows the blood vessels and thus acts upon the heart and circulatory system, raising blood pressure and increasing the respiratory rate.

2. Is cocaine addicting?

My answer, and that of many experts with experience treating cocaine abusers, is an unequivocal *yes*—if by "addiction" is meant an irresistible compulsion to use the drug at increasing doses and frequency even in the face of serious physical and/or psychological side effects and the extreme disruption of the user's personal relationships and system of values. When an addicted person tries to stop using the drug, withdrawal results. Cocaine withdrawal usually involves profound depression, irritability, sleepiness, loss of energy, and intense craving for cocaine.

It should be noted that some professionals do not believe cocaine to be addicting because terminating its use does not result in a physical withdrawal crisis such as delirium tremens (dt's) in alcoholics.

3. Why can some people use it without becoming addicted?

No one knows whether this is true. Some believe there is a so-called "addictive personality," but this is far from proven; some attribute addiction to genetic or biological differences among people, but again, this has not been established. It is because the causes of addiction are unknown and treatments are not curative that specialists believe that the only prudent course is to stay away from the drug entirely.

4. Is cocaine pure?

Street cocaine is almost never pure. It is mixed with a variety of substances to make it go further so as to increase dealers' profits.

5. Where do people get cocaine?

The most common sources, strangely enough, are friends and co-workers. It is not unusual, however, to get it at popular discos—remember the Studio 54 scandal of a few years back—or from dealers who hang out in city parks or in bars and restaurants across the country.

6. How can I tell if my child is using the drug?

If he or she suddenly becomes unusually secretive, shows extreme mood swings, loses interest in school and racks up large numbers of latenesses and absences, drops work or activities that had previously been absorbing, picks up with a new circle of friends, loses considerable weight within a short time, seems to be broke all the time and in need of more and more money, you may be observing the symptoms of coke use. Appendix C depicts paraphernalia associated with drug use.

7. I try to quit, but I can't; why?

Because quitting is extremely tough to do without help. You have to cut yourself off completely from the friend or friends with whom you've been using it, from the sources who sell it to you, and from the settings with which you associate its use. You have to substitute other activities and pleasures for the drug. All of this is hard to do without a support system and plenty of help. By the time you ask this question, you may be so addicted you need someone to help you obtain help.

8. How long does it take to get cured if you've got the habit?

There is no long-term cure. Rather, cocaine abuse is a chronic, recurring illness that can be controlled only by total abstinence from the drug. Medical evaluation and detoxification, or getting the drug out of the system, in a hospital setting, usually takes about a week or two. It's the treatment that follows, as suggested by the previous answer, that may take months, years, or a person's whole life.

9. My friend and I used the same amount of the same supply of coke and used it the same way. He got a buzz and I didn't. Why?

Essentially, because you're not clones of each other. You may metabolize substances at a different rate. Your nervous system may transmit messages to the brain more slowly. There can be a dozen different reasons. It is precisely because of these individual differences that your doctor adjusts dosages of antibiotics or other therapeutic drugs to your special needs.

10. I just had a seizure while on cocaine. If I use less, will it happen again?

It certainly can, no matter how little you use. This is one of the most serious side effects of coke use. Cocaine-induced seizures can and have led to death. Even one use in a seizure-prone person can result in a seizure. Continued use by anyone can lead to a reverse tolerance to the drug's seizure-producing properties. That is, less and less of the drug can induce seizures.

11. I use Dilantin to control the seizures I sometimes have because of epilepsy. Will the drug work to avert coke seizures?

No, it will not.

12. I am going for a life insurance physical. If they check for drugs, will they be able to detect coke in my urine or blood?

Yes, there are highly sensitive and accurate tests for this purpose—if the company employs these tests.

13. Is it true that cocaine can cause heart problems?

It certainly is since one of its actions is to narrow the blood vessels, which affects both the heart and the circulatory systems. It increases the heart rate, can cause heart palpitations, angina (severe pain around the heart), arrhythmia (irregular heart beat), and heart attacks.

14. How long does cocaine stay in the body?

Traces can be found for about a week.

15. I feel addicted, even though I only use coke two or three times a month. Am I addicted?

You've given the answer. If you feel addicted, you are addicted.

16. I am breast-feeding and using cocaine. Can the coke affect my baby?

Yes. Small amounts of the drug have been found in breast milk. You're definitely exposing your infant to the dangerous drug. Cocaine may interfere with nursing through its effects on the hormone prolactin. Cocaine use in pregnancy causes birth defects and developmental problems.

17. What can you do or tell me that will help me accept help with my coke problem?

My answer will sound like a copout, but it isn't. You have to believe that the drug is hurting you; that it is dangerous; that it is changing your life in ways that you can't stand; that it is hurting the people you care most about. A certain part of you has to want help. Only then can you be helped. Take the test in Chapter 7, and see where you come out.

18. How could a simple drug change my husband so? He is not the same person I married.

A drug that acts on the brain and changes the way a person thinks and feels is not a simple drug. Try to help your husband see that he needs help. While he's getting it, be as supportive as possible. If you're asked to participate in his therapy, do so.

19. My lover is using too much cocaine. What can I do to help him become a recreational user again?

Nothing. Clearly, your lover can't control his use. Usually people who ask this question are part of the problem. They do not know or cannot accept the reality that there is no such thing as recreational use of the drug—again. (How do you become a virgin—again?) Like an alcoholic who can't take just one drink without feeling compelled to take just one more, and then just one more until he's dead drunk, your lover has to become abstinent—or he will soon revert to abusing the drug.

20. Why can't doctors make up their minds? Is cocaine dangerous or not?
I know no doctor who thinks cocaine is good for you. And most doctors believe that too much of the drug can do you great harm. Where they disagree is on the question of whether it is addicting. I believe that the disagreement is over definition, as my answer to question 2 suggests.

21. One of my key executives has been missing more days of work and more deadlines than usual. I went into his office to leave him a message and found a mirror and razor blade with nothing on them on his desk. What should I do next?
Your colleague probably has a cocaine problem and may, in his own way, be calling for help. (The razor blade and mirror are used in connection with snorting the drug, see Appendix C.) You have to deal with him very sensitively in order to help him. For starters, tell him nonjudgmentally what you found and what you think it means. Offer to help him. Suggest that he talk to the head of the Employee Assistance Program if there is one in your company. If there isn't, tell him that you'll aid in finding a suitable doctor or program. Do not threaten or embarrass the person. Do not try to treat him. (Read Chapter 8, which goes into this problem in detail.)

22. I am using cocaine to stay thin. But now I really like it and need it. Is there anything else I can take to control my weight?
If you were thin before you started to use cocaine, you certainly don't need it to stay thin. Exercise and a balanced diet should help you maintain the weight you prefer. Get help from your doctor if you think you have a weight problem. But don't use a dangerous and addicting substance for this purpose. (If you are, you need help urgently.) That's like using an earthmover to dig a hole for a daffodil bulb.

23. Is cocaine really an aphrodisiac?
This is a question that has no one answer. Numerous drugs and

substances (for example, oysters) are alleged to be sex enhancers. Some users report that it heightens both their sexual desire and performance; some, that it has no effect on either. The mystique of the drug—that it is used by entertainers or jet setters at orgies— suggests to some that it is a sexual stimulant. On the other hand, men and women who use coke in large quantities report that the high is like an orgasm and is better than sex resulting in an orgasm. While its anesthetic effect may help to maintain erection, it may also decrease sensation. Women have told me that their partners become so self-absorbed when they have sex while on cocaine that they forget about their partner and her needs. All that can be said for sure is that coke is certainly not the universal aphrodisiac. And it may be conceptualized as a partner in masturbation.

24. One of my friends uses cocaine all the time. Can I get into trouble if she brings it into my house or leaves some in my car?

Yes. In many states possession of cocaine is punishable by law. Obviously, if you can establish that it was not yours and that it was left in your car without your knowledge or approval, you may escape punishment. But it may be hard to persuade a judge of your innocence or to persuade your friend to admit his guilt.

4
American Cocaine Epidemics: Then and Now

Most people have heard about marijuana, heroin, amphetamines, or LSD, and they may even have experimented with some of them, but until recently, the majority had not heard of cocaine being used as widely in this country as it is. It's almost as if an entirely new substance suddenly appeared from nowhere to provide yet another titillating drug experience. Oddly enough, however, we are now in the midst of America's second cocaine epidemic, the first craze having swept Europe and the United States in the 1880s when it was hailed as a medical panacea, good for curing anything from indigestion to nervous exhaustion. It was used by presidents, princes, popes, physicians, scientists, writers, actresses, and just plain folks, too.

For several hundred years after the Spanish carried reports of the plant, and the plant itself, from the New World to the Old, there was not much interest in it. Occasional published reports carried claims that coca allayed hunger, and imparted great physical strength to its users. Then, in about 1860, a German chemist, Albert Niemann, isolated the chemical we now know as cocaine from the leaves of the coca plant. About three years later, an enterprising French chemist from Corsica, Angelo Mariani, formulated a tonic, Vin Mariani, which combined a touch of cocaine with wine. A marketing genius before there was an advertising industry, Mariani pushed his product by sending samples of the attractively bottled and labeled elixir to eminent people throughout Europe and the United States asking only for a testimonial in exchange for a free taste. Apparently, few could resist a product that, as the label put it, "Nourishes . . . Fortifies . . . Refreshes . . . Aids Digestion . . .

Strengthens the System." In addition, it described the wine as "Unequaled as a tonic-stimulant for fatigued or overworked Body and Brain. Prevents Malaria, Influenza, and Wasting Diseases."

Testimonials soon poured in, ultimately a dozen volumes of them, from such movers and shakers and beautiful people of the day as Pope Leo XIII, President William McKinley, sculptor Auguste Rodin, writer Jules Verne, inventor Thomas Edison, actress Sarah Bernhardt, opera star Adelina Patti, and many others. Mariani's wine was sold through doctors; they drank it themselves and also prescribed it. Before long, there was a line of Mariani cocaine products that included teas and lozenges.

American entrepreneurs were not far behind. At about the same time, Parke-Davis, the drug company, marketed a variety of cocaine-containing products such as cigarettes, tablets, and sprays that were sold in drug stores. In 1886, a Georgia chemist, John Styth Pemberton, formulated a patent medicine and drink whose active ingredients were cocaine and caffeine.

He named the drink Coca-Cola. (Not until 1905 was the cocaine eliminated.) Thus, cocaine in wine was the drink of choice of upper-class Americans, while their working-class compatriots could and did by the tens of thousands get it in a variety of relatively inexpensive tonics and patent medicines. Cocaine as a mixer with whiskey foreshadowed the fashion that was to develop a century later.

Interest in the drug was not limited to soft drink and nostrum manufacturers. In the 1870s and early 1880s articles in respected medical journals in England, France, and the United States carried reports by physicians that were, on the whole, positive concerning the drug. They considered it effective in ending morphine addiction, a problem of some dimension at the time, and in treating various psychological problems. In addition, they confirmed the reports from the conquistadores that the drug warded off or relieved fatigue and hunger. Several called attention to the numbing effect of the drug on mucous membranes. The medical findings were widely disseminated in the popular press of the day.

The medical articles attracted the attention of a 28-year-old physician in Vienna who, in 1884, was struggling to make a name for himself. His name: Sigmund Freud. He was especially intrigued by the experience of a German army physician who reported that when he gave a few drops of cocaine in water to exhausted soldiers on maneuvers in Bavaria, their exhaustion disappeared within a few moments, their spirits brightened, and they continued on their long march. To test out the drug for himself, Freud began to take small quantities of it and to monitor its effects closely. He enlisted a number of his friends to join him in the experiment and to report back to him. Among these was 27-year-old Carl Koller, an ophthalmologist.

Freud's experience with the drug resulted in an article, *On Coca*, which was published in July 1884. It included a thorough review of the historical and medical literature on the drug, detailed his own reactions to it, and suggested various possible therapeutic uses from treatment of indigestion to treatment of morphinism. The last paragraph of the essay called attention to the possibility that the drug might be useful as a local anesthetic. The article received wide and on the whole favorable attention.

The reference to cocaine's possible anesthetic properties led to an experiment whose success marked a high point in medical progress. As had many doctors before him, Carl Koller had been searching for a local anesthetic to be used for eye surgery. Stimulated by Freud's comment, he decided to test out cocaine for this purpose. With a colleague assisting him, Koller mixed a solution of cocaine and water and trickled a few drops into one eye of a frog in a research laboratory. After a moment, Koller touched the frog's cornea with a sharp instrument. There was no reaction; the frog neither blinked nor recoiled. The same experiment was then carried out on other animals (and on himself) with the same result. Koller realized that he had discovered local anesthesia. When his finding was reported for him in October 1884, at a medical conference in Heidelberg (Koller was too poor to make the trip himself), it caused an immediate and worldwide sensation.

In the United States, one of America's most distinguished surgeons, William Halsted of Johns Hopkins, following the same lead, established cocaine's efficacy as a nerve block, and still another form of local anesthesia was discovered. (Unfortunately, in the process of working with the drug Halsted also began to use it. He became addicted, had to leave his work for a year to try to withdraw from the drug, was hospitalized for the problem, and eventually dropped cocaine—but then he became addicted to morphine.) In the next several years, Freud wrote additional essays in praise of cocaine.

However, several distinguished physicians of the day, almost simultaneously with Freud, began to report on the dark side of the drug. In Europe, highly regarded doctors disputed and refuted many of Freud's observations and recommendations. In the United States, too, medical reports of illness and death began to proliferate. In 1891 alone several hundred cases of cocaine toxicity and deaths are said to have been reported. For both altruistic and self-serving reasons (people were medicating themselves with cocaine instead of seeking medical assistance), doctors joined in a campaign to stem the tide of cocaine use. The drug was increasingly blamed for crime, for black men's attacks on white women (for which, of course, no evidence was presented), for deterioration of morale in the army and work force, in other words, for many of the real and imagined ills of society. Demand spread that its sale and use be restricted or prohibited.

Congress and the states obliged. Under the Pure Food and Drug Act of 1906, interstate shipment of products containing cocaine was prohibited, and labeling requirements on prescription drugs containing it became mandatory. A limit on the import of coca leaves was set for the first time. The various states began to pass restrictive laws as early as 1887, and 46 states had done so by 1914.

Then, in 1914, Congress passed the Harrison Narcotic Act (incorrectly including cocaine among various narcotics, since actually it is a local anesthetic and stimulant). The law required that distributors or producers of cocaine register with the government; that anyone involved in the lawful handling of the drug pay a special tax. There was also a record-keeping requirement. While possession was not illegal, it was considered evidence of a violation of the tax and regulatory sections of the law. Henceforth, cocaine could be purchased legally only for medical indications by a doctor's prescription.

In any case, for a combination of reasons, including high unemployment, a rise in the price of the drug, and experience with cocaine casualties, cocaine use declined sharply before World War I.

The first cocaine craze ended well before the Roaring Twenties began. Between the decade of bathtub gin and the pill-popping '60s, it virtually disappeared from public consciousness. Cole Porter's 1934 hit *I Get a Kick Out of You* nicely sums up the contemporary view:

> *I get no kick from cocaine*
> *I'm sure that if*
> *I took even one sniff*
> *It would bore me terrifically too*
> *But I get a kick out of you.*

By the 1970s, there was a strikingly different perception, as the lyrics of J.J. Cale's enormously popular song performed by Eric Clapton and entitled, simply, *Cocaine* demonstrates:

> *When the day is done*
> *And you want to run*
> *   Cocaine*

When you've got bad news
And you want to kick them blues
    Cocaine
Don't forget this fact:
You can't get back
    Cocaine
She don't lie
She don't lie

Dozens of other pop hits also conveyed the excitement of coke use, and most listeners, whether users or not, overwhelmed by the aura surrounding the drug, usually missed whatever warnings the songs contained.

Movies also reinforced the cocaine theme. *The* movie that brought coke to wide public attention is *Annie Hall*, released in 1977. In it, the quintessential schlemiel, played by Woody Allen, is offered some cocaine at a trendy, "in" party. The host explains that the white powder is worth $2,000 an ounce. Impressed, bemused, Woody wants to take a close-up look. He peers at the stuff in its jeweled case, sneezes—and blows it all over the place. Interest in the drug persisted, and in the first few months of 1982, for example, several enormously successful films featured it in one way or another. The plot of *Atlantic City*, starring Burt Lancaster, involved trying to get hold of a small package of cocaine that had disappeared. A Chevy Chase movie, *Modern Problems*, shows the star foiling attempts to make him powerless. He sniffs a white powder that instantly gives him superhuman strength. Audiences got the message that cocaine had done it. Finally, there was Richard Pryor's *Live on Sunset Strip* in which the appealing and brilliant star recounts his misadventure with coke. But there he is on screen— alive, whole, rich, successful. For many, the message must surely be "Use it; just don't get burned." Thousands listened, and this led to a new nonexplosive method for freebasing. Among the many messages in *Scarface* starring Al Pacino (and playing to huge crowds in 1984), is that coke dealing can buy gorgeous women, huge estates, and power. The kicker is you've got to stay alive to enjoy them—a problem in the dangerous world of cocaine trafficking.

In the real world, coke is ubiquitous. Scarcely a day passes without some news about a scion of a rich and famous family found with coke on his person and facing a jail term. Or that a Broadway star is fired, or a movie shooting goes over budget because of coke use by the cast. Or that four baseball players have been suspended for a year without pay for involvement with cocaine, following closely behind other tough actions taken against professional football and basketball stars.

But unknowns too, are involved, as any drug abuse specialist from New York to San Francisco can confirm. They represent the true cross section of the American middle class, as calls to 800-Cocaine make clear. The evidence from a variety of sources that follows substantiates that we are in the midst of a second cocaine epidemic far larger than the first. It is a public health and social problem of menacing dimensions.

• A 1982 National Institute of Drug Abuse survey of American households found that 21.6 million Americans—some one in ten of the total population—had tried cocaine, and that almost 12 million had used it in the year preceding the survey. The number of regular users (once a month) stood at about 4.2 million. It should be noted that the survey does not include members of the armed forces, or persons living in dormitories or in institutions of various types, or anyone younger than 18 years of age. It should also be kept in mind that some people, knowing cocaine is illegal, may be reluctant to admit experience with the drug. For all these reasons, these figures are probably on the low side.

The number of regular users could well be 4–5 million, a report in *American Medical News*, a publication of the American Medical Association, noted recently, while 10–20 percent of these could be drug dependent.

• A 1984 Gallup Poll of males 18 and older showed over 21 million had ever used cocaine, 7.6. million used in the past year and nearly 4 million were regular users.

• A Center for Disease Control 1982 report casts additional light on the dimensions of the cocaine problem. According to the CDC, more than 11,000 cocaine abusers (about 950 a month) were admitted to federally funded drug abuse programs in 1980, triple the number of just three years earlier. But this doesn't begin to tell the real story of the numbers of people who are seeking help for their coke-related health problems. Not included are those who turn to the 3,000 or more private resources that treat drug abusers, among them private hospitals, nonfederally funded clinics and support groups modeled on Alcoholics Anonymous.

The CDC also found a sharp increase over a recent five-year period in the number of emergency room admissions and the number of deaths directly related to cocaine abuse.

• Another deeply troubling finding, from the National Institute of Drug Abuse, is that about 16 percent of high school seniors reported in 1982 that they had used cocaine at some time. By 1986 it is expected that 20 percent will have used. In 1975, nine percent had reported doing so. Just under 12 percent in 1982 had used it in the past year, double the proportion in 1975. Finally, five percent in 1982 compared with two percent in 1975 said that they had used cocaine during the month before they were surveyed.

Since cocaine is expensive and teenagers generally neither earn high salaries nor have substantial income at their disposal, the question arises as to where they obtain the funds to buy the drug. Calls to 800–Cocaine have clued us in: Nearly one in six calls come from a teen or college student. Many teenagers phoned to say that they were in a panic because they were stealing from their parents, or dealing in coke, in order to get the money to buy it. They were terrified of getting caught and asking where to find help. Parents called to ask what they could do about their children's stealing from them, short of turning them over to the police. Teenage girls told us that they were becoming coke whores to acquire the drug.

• Still another indicator of the extent of the cocaine problem is how much of the drug is making its way into the country despite massive federal and state efforts to keep it out. Not surprisingly, the estimates vary. The official estimate of the National Narcotics Intelligence Consumers Committee is that in 1981 about 45 metric tons made it across U.S. borders. With record seizures by law enforcement in 1984–5 no one is quite sure about how much cocaine is actually coming in. Is it 50 or 100 tons? Since this was undoubtedly "stepped on" or adulterated many times before it reached the consumer, the volume actually available is enough to feed the millions of casual and compulsive users.

Another way of looking at what I believe to be a burgeoning and certainly major public health problem is to examine what is happening in a state that has excellent data on cocaine use. In 1981, New York State's Division of Substance Abuse Services (under the vigorous and committed leadership of Julio Martinez, its director) conducted a major telephone survey of a random sample of households statewide to probe the use of illicit and prescription drugs taken medically as well as nonmedically by residents aged 12 and over. The replies from almost 3,500 respondents were then projected scientifically to provide a picture of drug use among the state's estimated 14.3 million household residents. A similar survey had been carried out in 1975/1976, thus making it possible to see what happened over time in a population that included people living not only in New York City but in small urban centers as well.

The report emphasizes that "the findings must be considered low estimates of the actual numbers of users." Among the key findings are these:

• Cocaine is now the third most frequently used drug in New York State, with 477,000 residents using it in the six months prior to the survey.

• In the five years between the two surveys, recent cocaine use (use in the last six months) more than tripled. The number of people who had ever tried the drug doubled.

• An estimated 185,000 people in 1981 were new users of cocaine compared with 67,000 in the earlier period. One out of four residents who had tried the drug was a new user. (The report comments: "This suggests a phenomenon of epidemic proportions.")

• As to who in New York State uses the drug, the findings are strikingly similar to those of the hotline survey. Among both recent and new users, those aged 18–24 predominate while use by teens 14–17 dropped. It has remained about the same over time among persons aged 24 and over.

As for income, among recent users there has been a sharp decline in cocaine use among those earning $15,000 a year or less and a large increase among those earning $25,000 a year or more. (Seven percent of the state's residents earning $50,000 a year or more used cocaine in the six months prior to the survey, as did 26 percent of residents in low-income, single-occupancy hotels.)

Whites and males predominate among all types of users, although women are catching up.

• Frequency of use is an important measure of abuse. Among current users, about twice as many in 1981 reported use 10 or more times a month, compared with the earlier time period.

Increasing admissions to hospital emergency rooms and a larger number of deaths associated with cocaine abuse add further strength to my impression of a cocaine epidemic in this country. There is evidence both locally as well as nationally. Using reports from 46 hospitals in the New York metropolitan area, Mr. Martinez found that the number of cocaine-associated emergency room episodes increased as follows:

A 121 percent increase between 1979 and 1980; 17 percent between 1980 and 1981; and 47 percent comparing the first nine months of 1982 with the comparable period the previous year. All in all, from 1975 to the end of 1984 emergency room episodes have gone up an astronomical times. Since 1976, emergency rooms across the USA have exploded with cocaine victims: Atlanta (5 times), Boston (7 times), Buffalo (19 times), Chicago (15 times), Denver (12 times),

Los Angeles (12 times), New Orleans (180 times), Oklahoma City (20 times), St. Louis (8 times), and Washington, D.C. (12 times).

A similarly alarming picture emerges when cocaine-related deaths are examined. The number of such deaths in the New York metropolitan area increased 197 percent when 1980 is compared with 1979. In the San Francisco Bay area, a 300 percent increase in cocaine-related deaths has been reported over a recent four-year period.

By still other measures such as the number of felony and misdemeanor arrests involving cocaine, or the number of people admitted to drug treatment programs, the trend is the same—sharply upward.

Is the cocaine epidemic likely to persist? Or will it dissipate as the first one did? I believe that the bulk of the evidence points to a mounting problem, since the reduced cost of the drug is making cocaine available to an ever-increasing market.

With cocaine, use begets use. As the pool of users grows, more of the unexposed become exposed. This is because of the way cocaine is disseminated—from friend to friend, from worker to co-worker, from colleague to colleague, as our hotline survey, our professional experience, and anecdotal reports from other professionals in the field of drug abuse make clear.

Further, the major constraint on cocaine, as the users themselves report, is not ill health, although many of them are ill; it is not that they are destroying their families and careers, although they report that this is happening; it is not that they feel that their system of values has become distorted and subverted, although they say that this, too, has occurred. The main reason they consistently give is the high price of the drug. But the Drug Enforcement Agency notes that the price of the drug in the Miami area, one of the drug's main ports of entry, appears to have fallen, and a kilo is down from $60,000 in 1982 to $30,000 in 1983. We may well see expanding use and therefore expanding abuse.

One can only guess why the price may be coming down. There appears to be evidence that the amount of land devoted to cocaine cultivation has been increasing. As with other products, increased supplies may spell falling prices. For the cocaine users, this promises easier accessibility. For the American people, it forecasts even greater dislocations than are now being experienced.

There is no way to measure the human costs of drug abuse in general and cocaine abuse in particular. But we know it is tragically high.

If for no other reason than self-interest, it is essential to try to put a cap on the epidemic and to foster its eradication. A first step is to lay to rest the myth that cocaine is harmless. In the next chapter, I will show the suffering that cocaine can inflict on those who begin its use as a lark, for recreation.

5
Cocaine Can Kill

When I first met George L., he was 6 feet tall, weighed only 118 pounds, and looked like someone out of a concentration camp, or like someone dying of cancer. But when he pulled up the sleeve of his hospital gown, both his arms were covered from wrists to shoulders with needle marks. Dressings covered several of them. George was being treated for septicemia—blood poisoning. He became sloppy about cleanliness as he shot himself up with coke. He said he had been shooting it day and night for a month with just a few hours off for sleep, and almost no time out to eat. When he started to run a fever of 104.5° and passed out, he got scared. A friend rushed him to the hospital where the battle was on to prevent generalized septicemia, which, even in these days of miracle drugs, can be a killer. He was also being tested for hepatitis, a fairly common and serious complication of careless intravenous drug use. And the drip going into his arm contained a combination of vitamins and minerals needed to restore his body's chemical balance.

George's case history, in no way remarkable, is precisely what makes it so frightening. He was no deprived street kid looking to forget his ugly world. George is a typical American, brought up in an intact, church-going family, with father earning an adequate and steady living as a department supervisor in a mail-order house; his mother a homemaker and conscientious PTA member; two sisters and a brother from 12 years to 7 years older than he. George had been an average student, enjoyed team sports, had friends and the normal successes and failures with girls. As a high school freshman, he had tried beer for the first time; in junior year he had smoked some grass; neither alcohol nor marijuana interested him.

After high school, he went to work in an uncle's sporting goods manufacturing business, and within a couple of years he had proved to be both a good salesman and sales manager. So good, in fact, that by the age of 24 he was earning $31,000 a year.

Through business contacts, his world expanded, and he began to go out with a crowd that liked discos, health clubs, enjoyed good food and dinners in name restaurants. They all had cars, stereos, videotape recorders, were into skiing and scuba diving. It was not long before George was introduced to coke, not by a friend, but by a business customer with entrée to a cocaine club.

George hadn't known such places existed and was barely aware of cocaine. For business reasons he felt he could hardly turn down the customer's offer of a snort and at age twenty-five and a half, he was ripe for some excitement. He had been all work and ambition, was getting tired of his routine, had no really strong ties to anyone. Maybe coke would give him the shot he needed. The first snort was pleasant, but not remarkable. When he wanted to try it again, his customer-friend obliged with the name of his dealer and an invitation to a party at his home.

Then, as George tells it: "I would take some maybe once or twice a month. The more I used it, the more I enjoyed the high. Within six months I was buying about $100 worth once a week and spending my weekends snorting with a new set of friends. Then, someone told me about injecting it. At first I said no. I had always hated shots as a kid. But the truth was that I was ready for the next step. The rush was so wonderful, the feeling for the next half hour so great, I was ready for the next shot. Before long, I was buying $500 worth at a time and shooting it by myself. Still on weekends, but alone. I didn't want to be distracted from the great feeling by anybody else. Then, weekends weren't enough. I started to use it three times a week. Yes, I tried to limit it. I didn't want to go to work zonked; I noticed that I was tired and tense on the job, which I had not been b.c.—before cocaine. My boss asked whether I was okay, needed time off. I said yes, maybe a few weeks.

"But all I could think about was the drug. I wanted more of it more often. As a matter of fact, all I could think about was the next hit. Everything else seemed unimportant. I was spending so much for the drug I raided my bank account. Sold off stocks. When I ran out of money, I told myself I could borrow some from my firm. I had no idea how I was going to pay it back.

"From time to time, I was overcome by the thought that I was becoming a different kind of guy. I WAS STEALING. I WAS

LYING. But I couldn't stop. I knew I was losing weight. I couldn't sleep. I was beginning to vomit after every hit. I was getting more and more depressed. I began to think that the cops were after me or the dealers I owed more and more money to. I, who had never even thought about owning a gun, bought one to protect myself. I was hearing noises. Seeing shadows on the walls of my apartment. Then, one day I began to sweat all over; I felt so hot I thought I had caught fire, my heart was pounding. I passed out. When I woke up, I had just enough strength before blacking out again to call a friend. Next thing I knew I was in a hospital, things were being done to me. Maybe I was not going to die."

It had taken George just two and a half years to get from that first snort to the end of the line. He may be on the way to a fresh start if treatment works. The physical problems will almost certainly clear up. Even the paranoia and the hallucinations may come under control. The problem is whether George will be able to admit that he has a chronic illness with a high probability of recurrence. He will have to abstain for the rest of his life from the use of the drug he found so attractive. This is the hard part. His prognosis is uncertain.

In many ways, George's experience is typical of the experience of cocaine abusers. He started with occasional snorting, popularly considered risk free. Even among many physicians, there is an entirely mistaken notion that coke taken by this route is safe. It's not. Cocaine, by whatever route it's taken, is a powerful central nervous system stimulant. It constricts the blood vessels, increases the blood pressure and heart and respiratory rates, and raises the temperature. It acts directly on the brain. When it is snorted frequently and in substantial doses, it has highly destructive effects. It dries out the delicate nasal mucous membranes until they crack and bleed almost constantly. Home treatment of the nasal passages with vaseline or other oils or rinsing them with warm water has little effect if the snorting continues. Perpetual coldlike symptoms with constantly running nose are common, as is a condition of the frontal sinus that resembles sinusitis complete with a persistent dull headache. If minute amounts of cocaine are deposited on the nasal tissues and not completely absorbed into the bloodstream, it can erode the cartilage separating the nostrils (the septum), a condition requiring prompt surgical repair. I and many of my colleagues have referred patients to plastic surgeons for this condition, which once was regarded as extremely rare.

The vocal cords may also be damaged, causing permanent

hoarseness that a drug abuse specialist recognizes immediately as a side effect of cocaine snorting. I have personally treated pop singers panicked by the drug's effect on their vocal cords. If they seek help soon enough and quit using coke, their cords may in time heal.

Even the eyes may be affected, and it is not unusual for heavy snorters to report that they have become highly sensitive to light, or see fuzzily, or have the sensation that they are seeing floating objects out of the corners of their eyes, or see what abusers call "snow" lights, spots of lights in their central vision. They may even report double vision or image distortion in which objects appear smaller or larger than they really are. Again, the only cure for these conditions is nonuse of the drug.

At this point the reader might say to himself or herself, "Okay, snorting doesn't kill." Doesn't it? Here's an account given at a national conference on cocaine of a snorting-related death by someone with firsthand experience—Dr. Charles V. Wetli, Deputy Medical Examiner of the Dade County Medical Examiner's Office in Miami, Florida.

> "A typical cocaine death might be similar to that of a young girl's (aged 15) I autopsied who used cocaine rather infrequently. She went out one particular night to a disco party. She drank, snorted some cocaine, and then told her friends she wanted to lie down. She did that, had a small seizure, got up, snorted some more cocaine, and then lay down again. She soon went into violent seizures which literally threw her off the water bed.

> "Young people just don't die for no particular reason," Wetli commented. "The clues to her death, guiding us as to what to look for, were around her nose and mouth. She had some bloody mucous around her lower jaw and mouth, which came from biting the lower lip. Also her nose was filled with a white foamy froth—pulmonary edema fluid. The mechanism of death was centrally mediated respiratory depression, meaning that cocaine shut off respiratory control in the brain. Her breathing became very shallow, very slow, and stopped, while the heart continued to pump for a period of time. As a result the lungs filled up with blood and fluid, which literally percolated out of the nose and mouth. This is most characteristic of heroin, but

it can also be seen with cocaine, and we see it fairly frequently. Her lower lip had a tremendous laceration as a result of the terminal seizures, and her blood level of cocaine was approximately seven milligrams per liter, which is a fairly high level."

Dr. Wetli added that the young girl had also suffered an extremely high temperature (one of the common side effects of cocaine) which her friends had tried to bring down by placing her in a bathtub with cool water.

So much, then, for the view that snorting is risk free.

Even those who regard cocaine as a relatively benign drug view intravenous use with concern. Among abusers, the number of adverse and serious physical and psychological side effects is extraordinary, as the responses to the 800–Cocaine survey and George's experience prove. Chronic medical complications of intravenous use of cocaine, which doctors are seeing with increasing frequency, include (among others) various types of hepatitis, skin infections, and tetanus. A not uncommon condition, more often affecting men than women who shoot drugs, is *polyarteritis nodosa*, which involves inflammation and breakdown of medium and small arteries in the kidneys, muscles, gastrointestinal tract, and heart. There is increasing speculation that AIDS may result from unsanitary practices involved in shooting drugs, including cocaine. Finally, seizures are often seen in connection with cocaine use, by whatever route it is taken. It is of some importance to realize that they may occur in people who have never had even a single seizure before; of course, the drug abuser at highest risk of seizures is one who has epilepsy in any form. Epilepsy may be under perfect control because of the meticulous use of drugs prescribed to prevent seizures; but cocaine can and does overwhelm and negate the protection provided by these therapeutic agents.

The serious side effects specific to freebasing cocaine cannot be as well documented as those associated with snorting and injecting the drug because freebasing is a relatively new phenomenon. It is, however, known from the replies to 800–Cocaine and from clinical experience that the most serious side effects associated with the other routes also commonly occur in freebasers. In addition, it is believed that the capacity of the lungs to function efficiently may become seriously impaired, and that injury to the brain may become more common since a relatively large amount of the pure drug is inhaled and makes its way very rapidly to the various parts of the brain involved in reaction to the drug.

Heavy freebasers, like heavy injectors and snorters, often find the crash so unpleasant to tolerate, with its shakes and depression and extreme fatigue, that they may take the drug as often as every 10 or 20 minutes following the crash until their supplies (to say nothing of themselves) are exhausted. Or they may take the cocaine along with heroin (when injected in combination this is known as a speedball), which will bring on the euphoria and, they hope, prevent the side effects of the crash. Or they may drink heavily while doing cocaine for the same purpose. The consequences of these practices are even more destructive to the user.

Chronic abuse also results in a variety of dental problems, malnutrition, and sexual dysfunction (the very opposite of the aphrodisiac effect so commonly expected). A widely reported, but not proven consequence of cocaine abuse, is multiple vitamin and essential amino acid deficiencies. It made sense to us that this should be a consequence, given the fact that many coke abusers regularly neglect eating and suffer severe weight loss. A recent pilot study that we conducted documents the assumption that chronic and severe cocaine abuse does, in fact, result in multiple vitamin deficiencies. Using various tests, we drew a vitamin profile of each of 26 patients who came to us for treatment of their compulsive cocaine use. We tested for vitamins A, B_1 (thiamine), B_2 (riboflavin), B_3 (Niacin), B_6 (Pyridoxine), B_{12}, C (ascorbic acid), and folate.

We found that 19 of the 26 coke abusers showed at least one vitamin deficiency: 40 percent, of B6, and 23 percent, of Vitamin C. On the other hand, almost one quarter had higher levels than expected of Vitamin A, but this may be due to the fact that cocaine itself contains high levels of this vitamin. This observation on vitamin depletion, if confirmed, will aid in the medical treatment of cocaine abusers. In addition, 75 percent lacked an important brain nutrient, tyrosine.

We have already indicated that the respondents to our 800–Cocaine survey reported that they suffered, on average, 12 of a possible 21 psychological side effects of heavy cocaine use. This finding confirms a very widespread impression among those who treat cocaine abusers that they are at very high risk of mental illness.

One of the first signs of serious trouble is withdrawal from normal, everyday activities. Ambition and drive diminish and, over time, disappear. Relationships deteriorate. Values change radically.

The one drive that remains is to do coke night and day, and that calls for its acquisition no matter what the cost. The only relationship that counts is with the drug.

It is not unusual for a patient to tell me about sitting by himself in a darkened room freebasing, getting a brief high, followed by bouts of hoarseness and problems swallowing, feeling intense anxiety, knowing that his heart was racing, but nonetheless continuing to base until his supplies were gone.

A noted rock star I treated in an extended detoxification and rehabilitation program told me that he lived through just such a pattern, using cocaine continuously for 48 hours or more in a single binge. "I couldn't stop," he said, "anymore than I could stop breathing. I would crawl around picking up any grain that might have escaped. I wouldn't take calls. I left orders that no one disturb me. I missed taping sessions. I blew appearances. I stopped eating, shaving, washing, changing my clothes. I stank and knew I stank, but there was nothing I could do or would do except use up my coke supplies until they were gone." (He was experiencing, in short, what had been demonstrated experimentally in monkeys. Given a choice of food, water, activities they normally enjoyed, or cocaine, they chose the drug and continued to shoot it until they went into convulsions and died. They did not exhibit this extreme craving for any other drug offered them.)

Another rock star, an immensely gifted and attractive man, said that he spent well over a million dollars in one year on coke alone. He lost his homes, his cars, a collection of fine paintings, and eventually got his wife and daughter hooked. To support the family habit, he took to dealing heavily. This phase of his life ended when he was picked up by federal agents for dealing. He told us that this was the best thing that could have happened to him. "Otherwise my life would surely have ended as Elvis's did."

For the chronic abuser, as the hits become more frequent, as the binges continue for longer periods, what is often left is a psyche (as well as a body) in a shambles. A small sound magnifies into the delusion of a massed attack. A creaking drawer holds an FBI agent or a coke dealer with a knife aimed at the user's heart. A shadow on the wall is an enemy closing in.

What to do? Get a gun, a knife. Barricade yourself. Don't under any circumstances answer the phone. Someone has it bugged to take down your every thought, in addition to your every conversation. When the bell rings, be ready to attack.

This psychological condition is called paranoia. It can end in disaster as its victim acts on the false perceptions and irrational beliefs: running screaming into the street, shooting imaginary enemies, sometimes turning the gun on himself to escape the terror. Overdramatic? Calls describing these symptoms came into 800–Cocaine by the hundreds. Mental illness *is* bizarre. It can and does kill; cocaine can be the trigger.

As noted previously, deaths resulting from cocaine overdose are reported increasingly by medical examiners around the country. Fatal heart attacks, strokes, terminal seizures, asphyxiation, and suicide are the most frequent causes of death. It is important to remember that the people dying are those generally considered to be in the prime of life, men and women in their 20s and early 30s who would normally be described as having their most useful and happiest years still before them.

As I review the many ill effects that cocaine causes, I am more than ever convinced that the one side effect to fear the most is addiction. Antibiotics can usually take care of pneumonia and septicemia. Other medications can heal damaged livers and kidneys. Vitamins can replenish a starving body. But the causes and cure of addiction are still elusive. We are still far from certain what will guarantee a long-term cure, or who is sure to benefit from various therapeutic approaches. Becoming a cocaine addict is not like getting a strep throat. You can't take penicillin for 14 days and that's that. The problem is to help people recognize that there is no chemical solution to the challenges and problems of living. There is no quick fix.

6

Treating the Cocaine Abuser

Should cocaine abusers be treated as inpatients or outpatients? Or can some heavily dependent users just quit cold or by joining a support group like Cocaine or Narcotics Anonymous? Should the aim of treatment be complete and permanent abstinence from cocaine, or is controlled use a more realistic alternative? Is chemical intervention—the use of substances that block the effects of cocaine—a viable treatment alternative at this time? Can families or other loved ones assist in the treatment of coke abusers?

With treatment of cocaine abuse a relatively recent medical discipline—the current problem is about two decades old—it should come as no surprise that there is no general agreement on any one "best" method of treatment. From my personal experience, and from observation of the efforts of others involved in treating cocaine abusers, I am persuaded that there are four types of treatment that can wean abusers with various degrees of dependence from coke use. These include:

- Self-help alone;

- Joining a support group like Cocaine Anonymous;

- Becoming a part of a structured, supervised outpatient program;

- Signing in for inpatient treatment in a hospital setting.

The successful outcome of any of these rests on the assumption that the person recognizes that he or she is ill and that the cause of the illness is cocaine use. It then follows that permanent abstinence is essential for permanent recovery.

On the level of self-help, I have seen abusers, frightened by what was happening to their lives, take themselves in hand and quit without outside intervention. Eric, a college classmate of mine, is one of them. He happened to hear me on a TV talk show. One day later, he called me to say that he was afraid that he was becoming hooked, that cocaine was giving him the extra drive and energy he needed, that he enjoyed its kick, but he was using it constantly and was afraid that he was growing dependent on it. He had started doing cocaine about seven months earlier. He might, he told me, even be pushed into dealing. What should he do? I urged that he stop immediately, and make a contract, an agreement, with his wife that if he used cocaine one more time he would join a Cocaine Anonymous group. That was the end of the consultation. Eric did stop. Three years later he is still drug free. He has never slipped.

Joan, a 27-year-old Dallas stockbroker, needs more structured support to help her with her problem. For five months she had been sniffing coke, ever-increasing amounts of it, with her friends. When she realized that the drug was gaining control over her life and work, she told her husband about the problem. Together, they went to a psychiatrist who specializes in substance abuse for an evaluation. She was referred to a Cocaine Anonymous group, and six months later she is still attending the meetings faithfully. She is still off cocaine, and, as a matter of fact, both she and her husband have also stopped using alcohol. The usual vodka and tonic has been replaced with Perrier. Joan is on the way to kicking her habit.

I am less sanguine about a retail mogul whose conversation I overheard at a New Year's Eve party. It seems that he had been spending $1,200 a *week* on cocaine, and was growing so desperate about his inability to work or to think clearly that he "almost called" 800–Cocaine for help. Instead, he said that he resolved to cut down to $600 a week and to phase out slowly. Experience tells me he won't, that he will be among the millions of abusers who need but won't seek treatment until confronted by a crisis of enormous dimensions.

What Joan and Eric had in common, and the reason that they could be helped rather easily, is that their coke problem was of rather brief duration. They were regular users just on the verge of addiction who were able to admit what the drug was doing to their lives, and they had support when they decided to take steps.

Ellen F., however, came to us with a much more serious history of cocaine abuse. She told one of our psychiatrists that she could no longer control her twice-a-month coke use. It appeared that Mrs. F., an attractive, college-educated, 32-year-old homemaker, started doing cocaine about two years previously with a group of women friends who were her bridge companions two afternoons a week. A healthy, energetic woman, Mrs. F. found herself with too much time on her hands and not enough to stimulate her as she tried to meet her husband's demand that she concentrate on being his perfect companion and hostess. He was a highly successful investment banker, generous, loving, but totally involved in his career. When they married, eight years ago, Mrs. F. willingly gave up her burgeoning career as a TV reporter. Neither she nor her husband wanted children. She couldn't interest herself in community activities—so time hung heavy. There was only so much shopping, decorating, menu planning to do.

When her bridge friends offered her a snort, she accepted, titillated, a bit frightened, but feeling she was doing something trendy and socially acceptable in her general circle. In the past half year, purely social use had given way to private indulgence; Mrs. F. was doing coke several times a month—sometimes for four hours at a time. She was buying from a friend who was dealing to support her own habit and had dipped heavily into a small inheritance that she and her husband had agreed was hers to do with as she pleased. Now she was frightened. Coke had come to dominate her every waking hour. She feared she could no longer handle it.

A general exam showed Mrs. F. to be in excellent health, and while psychological tests indicated a somewhat fragile ego, she was certainly in no way mentally ill. When the staff reviewed her history, there was unanimous agreement that Mrs. F. was an excellent candidate for outpatient treatment. She recognizes and acknowledges that she has a problem with cocaine, an important first step, and agrees to twice weekly individual psychotherapy and participation in a group therapy program that meets four afternoons a week and Cocaine Anonymous meetings on "free days." The total program is to last six months. She is to agree to terminate all use of coke, and all other mood-altering chemicals including wine, alcohol, and marijuana, and to have her urine and/or blood monitored frequently to check on her cocaine status. (At her level of use, detoxification is unlikely to be accompanied by severe symptoms.) After some consideration, she is to commit herself to a contract with her therapist that specifies that if she fails to comply with every aspect of her program during the treatment period, she will agree to be treated in a more restrictive environment—that is, in a hospital.

From the above, it is evident that Mrs. F. can obtain care with a minimum disruption of her daily life. (In part, this is because of the availability within her community of the resources necessary to help her.) Were she working on a nine to five schedule, she could be channeled into an evening support-group program that meets four nights a week after dinner plus other free-night meetings. Key to weaning Mrs. F. from cocaine is her willingness to adhere to every aspect of her treatment plan. She will learn to anticipate, avoid, and cope with stressful circumstances or social pressures without drugs. Our experience is that men and women at this level of coke use have an excellent prognosis of recover. Our structured group outpatient program in Manhattan has a high success rate because of its ability to teach relapse prevention techniques and alternatives to drugs. (The cost of this type of outpatient treatment is roughly $100 a week. Usually, insurance does not cover outpatient treatment.)

But this form of therapy is not appropriate for the high-dose, frequent, compulsive user who can't admit that cocaine is the problem but who acknowledges that help is needed because he has had seizures, or paranoid episodes, or has been threatened with or has actually lost his job, or because his wife is threatening to leave him. The challenge in such a case is to get the abuser to admit that cocaine *is* the problem—and that all his other symptoms arise out of cocaine abuse. My colleagues and I believe that the first objective must be to get the addictive disease under control; therapy in this instance must take place in a hospital setting. Its outcome is much more problematic.

John H. was brought to the hospital by a "straight" friend who had spent the previous night with him in an emergency room watching him being treated for multiple seizures followed by bouts of vomiting. This was the fourth time in as many months that this had occurred. A doctor told John when he was stabilized that he had better get himself to a hospital for drug treatment because it was likely that the next time there was such an episode John could end up in the morgue rather than the emergency room.

This time he was sufficiently ill and disturbed to sign himself into the hospital. (He had previously been treated briefly by physicians for a variety of mental and physical problems, but not for drug abuse.) While the various medical, neurological, endocrinological, pulmonary, and psychological tests are under way and the results being evaluated, the patient provides a detailed personal, social, employment, medical, and drug history in a highly structured interview that usually takes several hours. John, it turned out, was the middle child of a middle-class family whose only problem was that the father drank too much on occasion. However, he was able to run his garment business capably enough so that it was one of the foremost in the industry.

John, a tall and quite handsome man of 31, chose not to go to college but to enter his father's business straight from high school. He learned it thoroughly from the bottom up and, like father like son, proved to be a brilliant businessman. By the time he was 25 he was earning well over $100,000 a year, was married to a pretty and intelligent woman with whom he had grown up, lived in a large home in an elegant suburb, and had a Mercedes for himself and a Triumph for his wife.

Despite all his accomplishments, John explained that he felt that he had done it all, had proved himself, and was merely running in place. Was this to be his life for the next 40 years, he wondered. The day before his 27th birthday, he was invited for a stag celebratory drink by a friend. He didn't much like booze, he explained to the psychiatrist, so one drink was enough. Then, a friend offered him a snort of cocaine. He had once tried marijuana and had taken amphetamines from time to time when he was in his teens, but he had found them unnecessary to his life. He'd expected the same reaction, that is, very little, to coke. His friend explained that this first reaction was not a fair trial. The next several hours were spent snorting. He called home to say he'd be out with the boys a while longer and wasn't sure just when he'd get home. His friend was right—the rushes got better and better; he felt that at last something could lift him out of his boredom.

Within a year, snorting escalated to a daily practice. Then came freebasing. Immediately before his admission he began injecting cocaine. He lost interest in wife, sex, work, anything unrelated to cocaine. The cycle was well under way. When his salary proved inadequate to support his habit, he spent his expense account money for the drug. His work performance dropped precipitously, and there were bitter fights with his father and between his father and his partners over what John was doing to the business. His wife left him. He no longer needed his home, he told himself, so he sold it. He was put on a leave of absence from the business—which suited him fine. Now he could really concentrate on what was important—coke.

It became his mistress, his boss, as he put it. And no matter what its demands, he met them. No matter how lousy he felt. And plenty lousy it was, he said—especially the seizures and the voices he couldn't escape.

John's workup confirmed his poor physical and mental health status. He could only be treated in the hospital, on the locked cocaine unit, which meant no coke at all. Reluctantly, he agreed to try it. (At this point, some patients simply choose to leave the hospital AMA—against medical advise—with a referral to an outpatient CA or NA support group.) The next five days were likely to be the most difficult John ever experienced. Without the drug, he became increasingly depressed, withdrawing from the world by sleeping 18 or more hours a day. Every time he woke up he thought about, tasted, smelled, and craved the drug. He was permitted no visitors and no mail—to be certain that no one slipped him any cocaine. He was searched to make sure that he had not somehow gotten hold of the drug. He had urine and blood samples taken to check on its level in his body.

During this period, he was not only being treated for any medical problems, but was communicating constantly with a psychiatrist with a view to his gaining the insight to admit that he had no control over the drug. The object: to force the patient to recognize that the drug had ruined his marriage, his business career, his health, his life. By the fifth day of detoxification, the patient is usually so irritable and nasty that interaction with the staff becomes extremely difficult. It is at this point that some addicts will persuade themselves that they no longer need help. They are no longer physically ill; they wear no scars. They feel that since they now know that coke is responsible for their problems, they can take control of their lives once again. Some, like John's roommate, Arthur, leave against medical advice at this point. Arthur declared himself cured after seven days in the hospital, although his cocaine addiction was of at least five years' duration. His preoccupation with the drug had changed him from a promising young physicist into a high school science teacher who deals in cocaine to support his habit. But the prospect that he will remain drug free, experience shows, is slight. It is such patients who may check into a hospital four or five times, repeat the detoxification period again and again, and resume the cocaine life.

In any case, John had enough insight to see that Arthur was just kidding himself. John was willing to admit that he continued to need treatment. (Meanwhile, John's workup, which had included an electroencephalogram and a CAT scan, showed structural changes with a minimal preexisting derangement of brain wave activity, indicating that he had an underlying propensity to epilepsy. Without cocaine, it might never have surfaced, but with the use of the drug it had done so. Now he was an epileptic. This disease is controllable with medication that he has to take for the rest of his life. He also suffered excruciating dental pain, had a serious vitamin deficiency, and appeared to have some lung dysfunction, probably as a result of freebasing. (His hallucinations and depression also appeared to be drug related, not neurological or psychiatric.)

After detoxification, John was again evaluated for his psychiatric status. Since there is no underlying illness, he will be able to participate in a 24-hour-a-day structured treatment program within the hospital. A highly specialized, multidisciplinary team will work with him, and he will join a peer group consisting of men and women who have been similarly detoxified but who are at different stages in the cycle of treatment. Such a group is especially valuable since it is familiar with what the cocaine abuser is going through, where he is coming from, and even what he is thinking at various stages. The verbalizations and interactions within the group often provide insight and relief for the entire group of patients and also point the way for the peer counseling staff and John's psychotherapist.

While this is going on, exploration is also under way, with John, about involving his family in the restructuring of his post-hospital life, about picking up once again with his drug-free friends, and about employment once he leaves the hospital. In John's case, his parents and even his wife were eager to help him, the latter only so long as he remained drug free. His wife and parents agreed to participate in family therapy with him while he lived in the hospital and after discharge if necessary.

Part of John's therapy is the successful completion of a drug information, addiction, and relapse prevention course, with mandatory readings, lectures, and examinations to make certain he is fully and correctly informed about the nature and history of his disease.

A comprehensive evaluation was undertaken with John to see how his leisure time outside the hospital could be restructured to replace the void left by the many hours he had previously spent in cocaine-related activities. It should be noted that recovering addicts report that they miss the comradely links to cocaine and the hours spent thinking about the drug, obtaining it, preparing it for use, and then using it. The post-hospital treatment plan must include enjoyable substitutes. We and many other therapists have found that a highly structured exercise program—running, dance, yoga, tennis, whatever the patient enjoys—not only makes it possible for the patient to concentrate his energies on nondrug-related activities but also puts him in touch with others who are also drug free.

Arrangements will be made with John for his participation over a considerable period of time (6 to 12 months) in a structured after-care program. The aim of such a program is to provide transitional and supportive care following the 24-hour care he received in the hospital. He contracts with the hospital to attend daily meetings on a certain schedule and to provide urine or blood samples for abstinence checking. Such a program, conducted by hospital staff, provides the swiftest possible feedback on the progress of the patient. Depending upon the need, home visits will be arranged, as well as intensive family and individual counseling. At the very least, such a program provides the possibility for social and recreational activities to reinforce distancing from the drug environment. The reason that John signs a contract to participate in such a program is that it compels him to think twice before violating it; the contract commits him to accepting hospitalization for a time if he violates any aspect of it.

When John reenters the world drug free, there are traps baited to ensnare him. He must learn where and what these traps are and to negotiate his way around them. To prevent a relapse, there are some resolutions he must adopt and stick to:

• He must avoid drug users altogether.

• He must not stay in a room or at a party where someone is preparing to use or is using drugs.

• He must not help friends find drugs or accompany a friend on such an expedition.

• He must not touch or handle any drugs at any time.

• He must not accept or fill any drug prescription without program approval.

• He must avoid going to places where he knows drugs will be available—a rock concert, for instance.

• He must realize that he can think about cocaine, crave it, but not use it. He must also realize that he is required to honor his outpatient treatment commitment in the face of all temptations and pressures to terminate.

A full-time job, leisure activities, a sense of values that recognizes that consumption is not the be-all and end-all of life (John *did* have the high salary, the cars, the home—they were not enough). Above all, establishing and cherishing relationships with loving others and a willingness to seek help at the first sign of temptation and compulsion to use the drug just one more time are essential to recovery. And acceptance of the view that drug addiction is a chronic illness with no cure—only remissions. In-hospital treatment nationwide ranges between $250–$500 a day. Most insurance contracts cover 80 percent after the deductible, but this varies from contract to contract.

Will John make it? Thus far, about one year after hospitalization, he is still drug free, still sticking to the regimen tailored to his specific needs. He gets tired of going to all the meetings but now knows he'd be lost without his new drug-free friends. We have found that the heavier and longer the abuse, and when the route is intravenous injection or freebasing, the lower the likelihood of permanent abstinence, which is the real measure of recovery. We estimate that about 50 percent of people like John make it.

In an effort to achieve a higher success rate, we (and other investigators) are researching the development of a nonaddictive substance that would block the drug's ability to produce euphoria. A former user who relapses while in therapy, for example, would find that he gets no kick out of cocaine. In effect, he is immune to the drug. He could be kept on the blocker until he gains the psychic strength to overcome the desire for and the drive to use cocaine.

Another avenue we are investigating is the use of the essential amino acids, tyrosine, tryptophan, and other chemicals like bromocriptine, to make detoxification easier for the patient; however, it is too soon to make definitive statements about their usefulness. Once we realized that chronic cocaine use decreased the essential brain messenger dopamine causing sexual malfunction, lactation and a syndrome like parkinsonism, we began trying dopamine augmentation in those patients with the most severe withdrawal and craving. Preliminary results with bromocriptine were very encouraging and reported by us in *The Lancet* in May 1985. Some researchers prescribe a variety of tranquilizers, stimulants, and antidepressants as part of ongoing therapy. Many drug abuse specialists regard such practices as controversial, possibly dangerous, and still to be proved effective in the treatment of cocaine abuse.

Also highly controversial is the use of contingency contracting as a key element in treatment. In Colorado, some therapists treating physicians, nurses, accountants, and other professionals, require that they write a letter to the appropriate licensing body in the state explaining that they have been abusing cocaine, have been under treatment, but have failed to remain drug free—and are, therefore, requesting that their licenses to practice be suspended or revoked. The letter is deposited with the therapist along with instructions that it be mailed if the patient fails to appear for a scheduled blood or urine test, or if such a test comes out positive. One study found that patients who signed such contracts remained abstinent much longer than those who refused to do so. To charges that the contingency contract seems coercive or Draconian, an investigator who uses this method is quoted in *Science* as saying that it is used primarily for drug abusers who "are rather desperate, who feel that they have lost control and need some type of external control."

The question of control is, I believe, central to the problem of treating the cocaine-dependent individual. The treatment objective is, in my view, to return control of his life back to him. This can be accomplished only if he truly accepts the view that cocaine is at the root of his loss of control over his life. That cocaine has induced in him a chronic, recurrent illness, the only relief for which is permanent abstinence from its use. While external controls may be useful tools in the course of treatment, in the long run what really counts is the self-understanding that culminates in the ability to live without resort to chemical crutches of any kind.

7
Test Yourself for Addiction

The symptoms of cocaine addiction are as plain to see as the signals warning that addiction is perilously close. The questions that follow spell them out in detail. Anyone who answers "yes" to as few as 10 of them is teetering on the thin edge of addiction. An affirmative answer to more than 10 is a clear signal that coke has taken over, that the user is addicted and is in urgent need of treatment if he is to have a chance to return to decent health and normal living. As a guide for anyone taking the test, we have provided brief explanations and comments to make clear why an affirmative answer means trouble.

Yes   *No*

—— ——   1. Do you have to use larger doses of cocaine to get the high you once experienced with smaller doses?
(This means you have developed a tolerance to the drug, that is, that you need more of it by a more direct route to achieve the same effect.)

—— ——   2. Do you use cocaine almost continuously until your supply is exhausted?
(This is called bingeing, and it signals loss of control over drug use.)

—— ——   3. Is the cost of cocaine the major factor limiting your use, and do you wish you could afford more?

(Your internal controls are virtually gone. The drug is in charge, and you will find yourself doing anything to get it.)

4. Do you use cocaine two or more times a week? (If you do, you are in the highest risk group for addiction.)

5. Do you have three or more of the following physical symptoms? Sleep problems, nose bleeds, headaches, sinus problems, voice problems, difficulty swallowing, sexual performance problems, nausea or vomiting, trouble breathing or shortness of breath, constant sniffling or rubbing your nose, irregular heart beats, epileptic seizures or convulsions?
(Three or more of these indicate severe loss of bodily function related to coke abuse—addiction.)

6. Do you have three or more of the following psychological symptoms? Jitteryness, anxiety, depression, panic, irritability, suspiciousness, paranoia, problems concentrating, hallucinations (seeing things that are not there), hearing voices when there are none, loss of interest in friends, hobbies, sports or other noncocaine activities, memory problems, thoughts about suicide, attempted suicide, compulsive, repetitious acts like combing the hair, straightening of clothes or ties, tapping the feet for no reason?
(Cocaine abuse is causing psychological problems that are not within the individual's capacity to control.)

7. Have any or all of the problems specified in the previous two questions caused you to stop using cocaine for a period ranging from two weeks to six months or longer?
(If not, the acquired disabilities are not strong enough to overcome the addiction.)

8. Do you find that you must take other drugs or alcohol to calm down following cocaine use?

(You are trying to medicate yourself so as to maintain your cocaine habit without suffering the terrible side effects of addiction. You are, of course, flirting with becoming addicted to a second drug.)

—— —— 9. Are you afraid that if you stop using cocaine, your work will suffer?
(You are psychologically dependent on the drug.)

—— —— 10. Are you afraid that if you stop using cocaine you will be too depressed or unmotivated or without sufficient energy to function at your present level?
(You are addicted and afraid of the withdrawal symptoms.)

—— —— 11. Do you find that you cannot turn down cocaine when it is offered?
(Use is out of your control.)

—— —— 12. Do you think about limiting your use of cocaine?
(You are on the verge of addiction and are trying to ration use of the drug.)

—— —— 13. Do you dream about cocaine?
(This is related to compulsive use and the total domination of the drug.)

—— —— 14. Do you think about cocaine at work?
(This is also a part of the obsession with the drug.)

—— —— 15. Do you think about cocaine when you are talking or interacting with a loved one?
(Obsession with the drug dominates all aspects of living.)

—— —— 16. Are you unable to stop using the drug for one month?
(This is certainly a sign of addiction.)

—— —— 17. Have you lost or discarded your pre-cocaine friends?
(You are stacking the deck in favor of cocaine by reducing negative feedback.)

—— —— 18. Have you noticed that you have lost your pre-cocaine values: that is, that you don't care about your job or career, your home and family, or that you will lie and steal to get coke?
(Addiction causes slow but steady changes in personality and the approach to life to reduce intrapsychic conflict.)

—— —— 19. Do you feel the urge to use cocaine when you see your pipe or mirror or other paraphernalia? Or taste it when you are not using it? Or feel the urge to use it when you see it or talk about it?
(This is called conditioning and occurs after long-term, heavy use.)

—— —— 20. Do you usually use cocaine alone?
(When addiction sets in, this is the pattern. Social usage ceases.)

—— —— 21. Do you borrow heavily to support your cocaine habit?
(You can be pretty sure you're addicted if you are willing to live so far above your means to get the drug.)

—— —— 22. Do you prefer cocaine to family activities, food, or sex?
(This is a sure sign of addiction. Cocaine need overrides fundamental human needs for food, sex, social interaction.)

—— —— 23. Do you deal or distribute cocaine to others?
(This kind of change in behavior signals addiction because it is an accommodation to the need for the drug.)

—— —— 24. Are you afraid of being found out to be a cocaine user?
(Addicts usually live a double life, preferring not to choose one or another alternative.)

—— —— 25. When you stop using the drug, do you get depressed or crash?
(This is a sign of withdrawal—a symptom of addiction.)

—— —— 26. Do you miss work, or reschedule appointments, or fail to meet important obligations because of your cocaine use?
(The drug has taken over your life.)

—— —— 27. Is your cocaine use a threat to your career or personal goals? Has your cocaine use caused you to lose interest in your career? Has cocaine caused you job problems? Has the drug caused you to lose your job? Has your cocaine use caused you to lose interest in or to have violent quarrels with people you love? Has your cocaine use caused you to lose your spouse or loved one?
(You would hardly sacrifice so much if you were not addicted.)

—— —— 28. Do people keep telling you that you are different or have changed in a significant way?
(Addicted people are indeed different from the way they were pre-cocaine. Such comments are a clue to addiction.)

—— —— 29. Have you used more than 50 percent of your savings for cocaine? Has your cocaine use bankrupted you and caused you to incur large debts? Have you committed a crime to support yourself and your cocaine habit? Have you stolen from work and/or family and friends?
(If you are not addicted, would cocaine be worth these dreadful problems?)

—— —— 30. Do you believe that your cocaine use has some medicinal value in treating a problem you have with energy, motivation, confidence, depression, or sex?
(Users who believe this are the most likely to develop addiction.)

—— —— 31. Do you think you have had withdrawal symptoms when you stopped using cocaine?
(Only addicted persons experience withdrawal.)

—— —— 32. If you had $100 to spend would you spend it on cocaine rather than on something for your house or apartment, on a gift for someone you love, on theater, records, movies, going out with friends or family?
(Addicts become so fixated on their drug they can think of nothing else, no one else, and no other form of entertainment.)

—— —— 33. Do you think that you are addicted?
(If you think so, you probably are.)

—— —— 34. Do you use cocaine compulsively despite your recognition that the drug is a very real threat to your physical and psychological well-being, relationships, family, and job?
(This is addiction.)

—— —— 35. Did you ever enter psychiatric treatment or therapy for a cocaine-related problem and not tell the doctor or therapist about your cocaine use or how current or recent it is?
(When an addicted person is pressured into getting help, he may not only try to cover up the extent of his drug abuse, but may also use his treatment as a cover for his continued use of the drug.)

—— —— 36. Did you have a cocaine problem that was cured either through your own efforts alone or with the help of friends or with professional treatment?

(The critical word is "cured." No addict is really cured—rather, he has a remission of a chronic disease that can recur should he become a user of cocaine again.)

37. Have you ever used cocaine and had hallucinations, a convulsion or seizure, angina (severe pain around the heart), loss of consciousness, the impulse to kill yourself or others? And when any of these side effects passed, did you figure that you would use less next time or use a purer quality of the drug?
(These side effects are related to addictive use, but the addict prefers to ascribe them to overdose or to the adulterants used to make the drug go further. He then can continue to use the drug under the illusion that it will be okay the next time.)

38. Do you leave paraphernalia or a supply of cocaine at work?
(This may be a call for help by a person who feels that his life is out of his control. It is like a suicide note left so that people will find it and prevent the act.)

39. Do you sometimes wish that you would be discovered as a user by someone who would see to it that you got into treatment and recovered?
(If so, you know you need help and want it.)

40. Do you use cocaine three times a week or even more often, and still try to maintain an interest in diet, health, exercise, and fitness?
(The interest may be there, but the fact is that such heavy use of the drug makes it virtually impossible to act on the interest. There is too great a conflict in values.)

41. Have you switched from intranasal use to freebasing or intravenous use?
(This usually means that tolerance to the drug

has developed, and it is very likely that you will binge and become addicted in short order.)

—— —— 42. Have you been using cocaine more than once a week for three or more years?
(With this much use, any stress, or change in your life, can turn you into a daily user with a high probability of addiction resulting.)

—— —— 43. Do you find yourself choosing friends or lovers because of their access to cocaine or their cocaine use?
(This kind of behavior usually indicates a life out of control.)

—— —— 44. Do you wake up in the morning and wonder how you could have let cocaine gain control over your life?
(You are addicted if you have these thoughts.)

—— —— 45. Do you find it almost impossible to fall asleep without a drink or sleeping pill or tranquilizer?
(You now have a second addiction.)

—— —— 46. Since you started using cocaine, have you ever wondered whether you would be able to live without it?
(We find that people who raise this question are generally hooked on the drug.)

—— —— 47. Have you wondered whether you would be better off dead than continuing to use cocaine?
(This question usually suggests an addiction so profound that the addict feels himself terminally ill.)

—— —— 48. Have you ever wished that you would die of an overdose in your sleep?
(Same as above.)

—— —— 49. Do you use cocaine in your car, at work in the bathroom, on airplanes, or in other public places?

(You are so desperate you want to be caught—
and helped.)

50. Do you use cocaine and then drive a car within
six hours after use?
(Cocaine has impaired your judgment and you
are out of control. Don't wait to get help until
after you have impaired or killed a pedestrian.)

8
Coke in the Workplace

He sits at his desk, a phone cradled between chin and shoulder, scribbling notes as he listens. The moment he hangs up, a young colleague walks through the open door, is greeted with a smile by the boss, and is waved to a chair next to him—not across the desk—but next to him. After a moment's banter, they examine some papers together, talk about the matter at hand for about 10 minutes, and then the younger man leaves.

An instant later, the older man is on the phone again. The conversation over, he gathers up some papers, glances at them, and is on his way to a management meeting.

As he makes his way to the conference room, he smiles and waves to co-workers, stops at a desk for an instant to chat. It is clear who Ken W. is and what people think of him. He is an upper-middle manager (in one of America's largest insurance companies), self-confident, poised, pleasant, a man who knows every one of the people he supervises, respects them, and is in turn respected by them. At age 44, he has the look of a successful man content with his life. A man who seems to have escaped the destructive features of the rat race. Right? No. *Very wrong.*

Ken has been to hell but was hauled back because someone cared enough about him to throw him a good strong lifeline.

This is his story. And this is the story of a program that sees the thousands of employees of large companies as individuals who, when they come to work in the morning, bring with them not only the assets that landed them their jobs but also the liabilities, the burdens that go along with being human.

Ken was recruited into his company the spring he graduated

from the state university where he was a straight B student, active in the student government, and on the swimming team. The recruiter recognized in the young man the almost indefinable quality of leadership potential that his company was looking for in young people. For his part, Ken had talked with other recruiters, had considered other firm offers, but none had all the pluses of company X. It was located in the capital of a small New England state that had real country all around it, not just suburbs. It was a town in which you could make a difference if you chose to participate in local government, and where you could find good skiing in an hour. Although he expected to and would start at the bottom of the executive training program, the pay was not bad, and the chances for promotion were good. Ken signed on, age 22, and within two months married a young woman he had been going steady with since junior year.

The company was right about Ken, and Ken was right about the company. They suited each other to a T. Within 10 years, he was a middle manager with more and more responsibility. He brought in millions of dollars of insurance business, almost effortlessly, it seemed. And he proved to be an excellent supervisor, his unit among the most efficient and effective in the company. By that time, he was the father of much loved nine-year-old twin sons. Despite the bulging briefcase he brought home almost every night, he somehow found time to take his family on camping trips into the nearby mountains, to play tennis several hours a week with his wife and another couple. And he was elected to the town's budget and finance committee where his knowledge and commitment were valued. Promotions kept coming, and at 40 he was one of the youngest assistant VPs in the company.

Then his world began to fall apart. His wife was operated on for breast cancer, had a difficult time with chemotherapy, but, the doctors said, stood a good chance for a full recovery. His children were off to college in the Midwest, leaving behind a very empty nest. And, for the first time, he was passed over for a promotion he felt should have been his. Added to this was the 40s blues—he didn't feel young anymore, he had added a few extra inches around the waistline, couldn't play as much tennis as he liked, and, to cap it all, found himself less interested in sex.

He was a prime candidate, in his state, for cocaine, and good friends saw to it that he got some. Ken, who had avoided drinking because he had firsthand experience with a parent who was a recovering alcoholic, was captivated by the drug. It provided just the lift, the feeling of self-confidence that he needed. Within two years, the drug was his life. Despite the pleas of his wife, who refused to share his coke pleasures, he was spending most of his pay to buy cocaine. Then he dipped into their savings more and more deeply and cut himself off from most of their straight friends. His briefcase was left unopened most nights. Monday mornings he could hardly make it to the office, and often did not. He lost weight. He also had little interest in or patience with the job and the other people who depended upon him for leadership.

Early on, his breakdown was observed by his colleagues. The executive to whom he reported noted in his formal evaluation that Ken's work had deteriorated sharply, that he was taking an inordinate number of sick days off, that he had become uncharacteristically short-tempered with his co-workers, and that he had grown untidy in his appearance. He was asked whether he needed help and was told that the company stood ready to help him. No, he didn't, he insisted. He could handle his problem by himself, as he had always done.

Then, large premium checks that crossed his desk began to disappear. This time, his supervisor said that unless he reported to EAP—the employee assistance plan—for help, his job would be in jeopardy. There was no time to waste. Ken, with much hostility and little confidence in what was going to happen to him, grudgingly made an appointment with a counselor in the program. Together, they reviewed his current employment history. With some reluctance, Ken agreed that he was in trouble and blew the whistle on himself. Out came the story of his personal and family problems, of his drug abuse. The counselor explained that the company was prepared to refer him for help to the best program in the area. They continued to value him, would not fire him, but would restore him to his position if he went into therapy and continued it until his physical and mental health were restored.

A proud man, Ken wondered whether everyone in the company would learn about his problems, whether his treatment would be kept confidential. Assured that it would be, he took a leave of absence, was checked into a hospital for diagnosis, detoxification, and treatment. It was a tough course for this in-charge kind of person. He felt ready to leave the hospital as soon as he had been detoxified. He didn't, however, and began to participate in individual and group therapy in the hospital. Eventually, his wife joined him in family sessions.

In three months' time, Ken was back at his job, looking more fit and behaving more like the person everyone had once known and respected. But his life was not exactly the same. Every evening for the next six months, he attended group sessions at the hospital, and provided urine samples as a check on his drug status. With his wife's help, he dropped his cocaine friends and began to rejoin his old circle. Once again, tennis and swimming (now part of his recovery program) became regular features of his life. Therapy helped him confront and deal with the fact that although he was no longer young, he had many years of opportunity and accomplishment before him, and that diminished sexual activity at his age was completely normal.

Within a year after his return to his job, he earned a promotion. By this time, Ken was working three evenings a week as a volunteer drug counselor at the hospital and was, and remains, one of the most effective the institution has. He knows that he isn't cured, that he has a chronic illness that will recur if he tries even one snort of coke.

Ken's career was saved by the intervention of his company's Employee Assistance Program. Such programs are now a feature of health benefit packages of many large companies; six years ago, 56 percent of the Fortune 500 companies had EAPs. Many more have them today. Among the best are: the Equitable Life Assurance Society of the U.S., Reynolds Metal, General Motors, Johnson & Johnson, Kimberly-Clark, AT&T, Prudential-Bache, Nabisco, American Express, NBC, Bell Laboratories, Western Union, Merck, Conrail, TWA, United, Merrill Lynch, New York and New Jersey Bell.

Although altruism may be part of the reason for such programs, most are in place for hardheaded business reasons. It costs less to treat and rehabilitate an efficient and valuable employee than to recruit, hire, and train a new one. A recent report found that for every $1 companies invest in such programs, they save from $2 to $5—a fine return from any point of view.

Three years after adopting an EAP (now considered one of the best in all America), AT&T evaluated its impact both on the employees who sought help and on the company. The study found that the major problems for which treatment was sought were alcohol and drug related, followed by emotional, family/marital problems, and work-related problems. As with Ken, the vast majority of employees were referred for care outside the company with the EAP counselors providing follow-up services and keeping in close touch with the treatment program. The outcome of the assistance provided could not have been more gratifying for the employees or the company: Eighty-six percent were found to be wholly rehabilitated—meaning "restoration to a former state of health and efficiency"—or improved. The category in which the greatest degree of rehabilitation was found was for alcohol- and drug-related problems.

A vast improvement in performance and sharp reductions in absenteeism, disability leave, accidents on and off the job, and visits to the company's medical department occurred following treatment, resulting in minimum saving to the company of almost half a million dollars. Among men and women referred for help because they were performing poorly and were in jeopardy of losing their jobs, more than 85 percent were no longer performing poorly following EAP intervention and of these, 41 percent was promoted following care. Ken's experience, therefore, was not the exception.

With alochol and marijuana, cocaine has become a prime drug to use at work. It is available, easy to conceal, fast acting and hard to diagnose. It is a contagious disease at work with one user influencing 3–10 others. Cocaine abusers constantly send out signals to their colleagues and supervisors, which, picked up and acted on promptly and with sensitivity, can lead to restoration of pre-cocaine behavior, health, and values. On the job, the signs to look for are erratic or unusual behavior; failure to meet schedules; missed appointments; increasing lateness and unexplained and lengthy disappearances in the course of the workday; irritability, negativism, and constant arguments; sharp mood swings and decreased energy and confidence. People abusing cocaine generally care less about their personal appearance and hygiene. However they always seem to be having physical problems, and going to physicians. They usually lose their former competitive spirit, seeming not to care anymore about promotions. In this connection, they may even ask to be demoted and to work in more isolated areas (to avoid observation). They take more and more sick leave, and when confronted with poor performance, they may ascribe it to poor health.

Supervisors who observe such changes can be helpful to the troubled person in various ways. They should:

• Document work-related lapses.

• Discuss these at the earliest possible moment with the person involved.

• Suggest that there is help available and offer to refer the person to the appropriate official in the company.

• Make clear that the job will be in jeopardy unless the behavior is changed and performance improved.

Under no circumstances should supervisors diagnose what is causing the problem. They usually have no proof and are unqualified to do so. For the same reasons, and despite good intentions, they should never try to be therapists. Finally, moralizing is offensive, useless, and a waste of time. A cocaine abuser is sick, not depraved; he or she needs help, not sermons. In my experience, people with serious cocaine-related problems will often accept offers of help, especially when their jobs are on the line.

On the other hand, overprotectiveness by colleagues and complicity with the drug user can delay treatment beyond the point when recovery is a possibility. I have worked with actors and prominent singers whose managers thought it more prudent to keep their clients supplied with drugs than to help them with their problem. Cancelled or bungled tapings, missed performances, and, eventually, fewer and fewer bookings were the common outcome of such poor judgment.

Many of the entertainers I have treated told me that there was often someone in their entourage whose sole job it was to obtain supplies of drugs and to take the rap for dealing or being found in possession. In exchange for this "service" huge amounts of cash went from performer to lackey. Bail and legal expenses were paid whenever necessary. With pals like this, the entertainer needed no enemies. Years of struggle and widely acclaimed talent are sacrificed because of the failure of colleagues to take positive steps to get help.

The ultimate loser in the drugs-in-the-workplace phenomenon is the public. The public pays for the car brakes that don't work properly; for the clothing seams that rip open after three wearings; for the doctor's error when he writes a faulty prescription; for the failure of the policeman to answer calls for help because he is impaired; for the sloppy workmanship of personnel in nuclear plants; for the stockbroker who fails to make a transaction or makes the wrong one.

We are all endangered and/or cheated unless we are aware of and know what to do about drugs in the world of work.

9

How We Can End the Epidemic

Daddy returns home from work, wrung out after a stressful day at the office. When the kids hear the key in the lock, they run to the door to greet him. They fling it open, he smiles at them, puts his hat on one, hands his briefcase to the other, and after a few hugs, announces, "Boy, do I need a drink!" To the kids aged 8 and 10, this means Dad had a tough day and needs to relax. Sprawled on the couch with a drink in one hand, a cigarette in the other, he fools around with them. Everything is as it always is.

At dinner, Mom and Dad debate whether to have a red or a white wine with the pork roast. Smiling at each other, they compromise on a rosé. Each has two glasses with dinner. The whole family pitches in to clear the table, load the dishwasher, store leftovers in the refrigerator.

Then, they move to the den to watch some TV together. At the first break, Dad and Mom share a cool beer. The program over, the kids are urged, cajoled, and finally ordered to bed. Grown-up time has arrived.

The parents return to the den. Mom flops down next to Dad, exclaiming, "Ugh, what a day. I rushed home from work, got dinner going, kept the kids from killing each other, supervised homework, worried about my presentation for tomorrow's important meetings. I'm exhausted. Do me a favor, sweetie, get me a Librium."

No one gets drunk, no one gets high, no one gets spaced out, no one has broken any laws. This is 100 percent, middle-class, everyday, okay behavior, isn't it? The answer is yes. And two small children have learned that booze and beer and wine and cigarettes and tranquilizers make their father and mother feel good, help them cope.

The scene changes. The kids are now 13 and 15. They're trying to cope, too, with lots of new stresses. How to be grown up ("Act your age," the parents' refrain), how to handle the enlarged world of junior and senior high school, how to deal with the need for independence, with sexuality, with greater intellectual demands. A friend at school offers a puff of grass between classes in the schoolyard. Nice. It makes you feel good, less hassled. The scenario is virtually written. The kids are on their way to the chemical solution. Your kids, my kids. And they start young. Here's how many were estimated to be using one drug or another at ages 14–15 in 1982, according to the National Institute of Drug Abuse:

- Marijuana—640,000

- Cocaine—100,000 (and this is the world's most expensive drug)

- Stimulants (Dexadrine, Benzadrine, Dexamil, etc.)—100,000

- Sedatives (Quaaludes, Seconal, Nembutal, etc.)—50,000

- Tranquilizers (Valium, Librium, Benadryl, etc.)—50,000

- Alcohol—1 million

- Cigarettes—740,000

The use of these drugs keeps rising during the teen years to that among 16–17-year-olds, for example, about 2 million use marijuana regularly, 260,000 "do" cocaine, about 3.4 million are drinking alcohol, and 2.5 million are smoking. (A grand total of about 190 million Americans aged 12 and over use these drugs either separately, or in combination.) The National Institute of Drug Abuse estimates that about 80 million Americans have used marijuana and cocaine. Since the recent national survey has shown that among all adolescents who had *ever* tried cocaine, only 2% never used marijuana; prevention means decreasing and eliminating teenage drinking, cigarettes and marijuana smoking.

A question I'm often asked is where teenagers get the drugs and the money to buy them. My answer is usually a shocker: They get most of the drugs out of the home medicine cabinet and the family bar, or from friends with similar access. After all, stimulants, sedatives, and tranquilizers are legal and useful when taken as prescribed. There are 20,000 psychoactive drugs available in the United States, and more than 20 billion doses of them are distributed legally each year. We are a drug-using society, and a drug-abusing one as well, what with 11 million alcoholics, at least three million narcotic and nonnarcotic abusers, and uncounted millions of nicotine abusers.

As for marijuana and cocaine, teenagers can often buy them on the school premises from fellow-students, or in nearby parks and teen hangouts. Recently, there was a drug bust in the high school in the upper middle-class suburban community where I live and work. Sixteen students were suspended. The money for the drugs generally comes out of the allowances and gifts middle-class America gives its children, and out of the wages some of them earn on after-school, weekend, and summer jobs. If the habit gets compulsive enough, they deal and steal, as many calls to 800–Cocaine from frightened and tearful parents make clear.

Can anything be done to stem the drug abuse pandemic? Without suggesting that it will be easy, or that the efforts will all be successful, I think that there are steps that can be taken at least to stem drug abuse.

A first step, and perhaps the most important one, is for each of us to admit not only that there is a drug problem but that we are part of it.

We parents of today's young teenagers were around 15 in the mid-1960s, at the time of the drug explosion that paralleled the Vietnam protest movement and the rejection of middle-class values. At the very least, many of us tried a joint from time to time, attended the Woodstocks around the country, bought the records, and sang the songs that condemned hypocrisy and glorified alternative lifestyles and mind-expanding and mood-altering drugs.

As time passed, many of us rejoined middle-class America, adopted its lifestyle. Drinking is not only okay, it is virtually mandatory. The occasional joint is stylish. So stylish that, according to a December 11, 1983, report in *The New York Times*, "marijuana is currently our second-largest cash crop nationally, after corn." Heroin and LSD, no, those are for slum dwellers and far-out freaks. We have learned to handle pressure, loneliness, frustration, and aging with legally prescribed psychoactive drugs, which we misuse and abuse.

Many of us, and our younger contemporaries, beguiled by the behavior of the beautiful people, the rich and the talented, flushed (and under constant stress) by our own developing success, are trying and becoming hooked on cocaine. We may even use cocaine and marijuana or cocaine and alcohol at the same time. We are accustomed to living way beyond our means. We flesh out our domestic economy with loans and credit cards. So it is almost a natural extension of this logic that we can live outside our emotional means, with drugs, and get away with it.

Against this background, it is not surprising that so many of our children, and our younger contemporaries, turn to drugs rather easily. So, it is up to us to reexamine our behavior and to start communicating honestly with them about drugs. Like sex education, drug education should begin at home. And the earlier the better, since our children begin drug experimentation when they are still in elementary school. More than one in three students try an illicit drug, other than alcohol and marijuana, while they are in high school, and more than one in three regularly abuse drugs other than alcohol. In this connection, it came as a shock to me, an expert in drug abuse, to realize that in the past year or so I had heard from about 10 percent of my own high school graduating class who were seeking referrals for drug abuse treatment! Without exception, these were the children of middle-class parents whose main aim in life was to provide their offspring with the best that America has to offer its young. Parents should start with themselves, and then move on to stop providing excuses for smoking and providing drinks for teenagers.

The second step is to involve ourselves in or to initiate community efforts to deal with drug abuse. PTAs, which are not without clout, should press for drug education (as many have for sex education), preferably integrated into as many subject areas as possible. English and American literature, social studies, biology, chemistry, and health education could certainly accommodate aspects of drug education. In-service training programs for teachers should be organized to help them become effective leaders in the undertaking.

In addition, community efforts on drug abuse should include the broadest spectrum of professional, social, fraternal, and civic organizations. Doctors, nurses, social workers, businessmen, clergymen, and representatives of the police and court system are among those who can be helpful.

Most important, students themselves should be encouraged to become participants in community efforts and to assume leadership roles, since peers will often be more effective than adults in communicating with their friends. It's well known that peer pressure plays an important role in enticing youngsters into drug use in the first place. And they can help educate adults about why and how their contemporaries become involved with drugs.

Finally, as parents and teachers, we have an obligation to recognize and act on the earliest symptoms of drug use and abuse by our children. Waiting until the child falls apart makes treatment all the more difficult and outcome questionable. Denial that there is a problem only delays its resolution; it is not likely just to disappear. As nonjudgmentally as we are able, and without theatrics, accusations, and recriminations, we should discuss what we have seen or found, and work out a plan of action, making clear what is expected.

A youngster should know that if he drinks, smokes grass, or snorts cocaine, he will not be permitted to drive the family car; not only because he may endanger his own person but because he may be a menace to others on the road. (The leading cause of death among 15–24-year-olds is accidents which result from driving while under the influence of alcohol.) Also, he or she should not play on a school sports team until absolutely clean.

The adolescent must understand that if he or she is involved in a drug bust, or in dealing drugs, or is in danger of suspension or expulsion from schools, the parents will cooperate with the authorities in dealing with the problem and will not act in complicity to beat any raps. Parents should indicate a desire and willingness to obtain therapy as a family if that seems necessary.

And, although it should not be necessary to say this again, parents must forego the pleasure of abusing drugs themselves. If moms and dads use illicit drugs, such as grass or cocaine, and misuse psychoactive prescription drugs, the message transmitted to young people is "Do as I say and not as I do," and is perceived as the double standard that it is.

I am constantly amazed at how casual some law-abiding, well-educated men and women I know are about obeying drug-related laws. My wife and I were not invited to a friend's housewarming party because, as his wife explained, she knew that most of the guests would use grass and coke during the evening, and she didn't want to embarrass them or me. (Among the guests would be several physicians.) I suggested that she explain to the others that since I was coming to the party they should leave the stuff at home. She explained that she couldn't do that because that would be an infringement on their personal rights! The fact that they were indulging in illegal behavior, and were placing those of us who were in no way involved in drug use in legal jeopardy in the event of a bust, was not persuasive to her. She was also fearful that I might report the drug-abusing doctors to the Impaired Physicians Committee.

It is highly unlikely that the children in such households don't pick up these confused and confusing messages.

There is much to be done in the arena of public policy where laws relating to drug abuse are either a hodgepodge that make little common sense or are years behind the reality of drug abuse in general and cocaine abuse in particular. Appendix B is a table of penalties for possession, trafficking, and use of cocaine, by state.

In an attempt to reduce the slaughter on our highways attributable to alcohol abuse, some states now commonly mandate breathalyzer tests for people suspected of or observed driving while under the influence of alcohol. There are few similar laws requiring blood or urine tests of drivers who might be under the influence of drugs, although such tests are available, accurate, and relatively inexpensive. (Some states do have implied consent provisions that permit a police officer to require a driver to submit to a blood test.)

One such law has been under consideration by committees of the New Jersey state legislature for several years but has not yet made its way onto the floor for general debate and consideration. The law requires revocation of a driver's license for varying periods, and fines up to $500 for anyone who refuses to have these tests made. (Recognizing that driving a car is for many people an economic and practical necessity, the law permits driving to and from work and for marketing and medical care. Persons found driving outside the hours when such tasks are normally performed are subject to stricter limitations.) How urgently such laws are needed is highlighted by the fact that fully one-quarter of the 500 respondents to the 800-Cocaine survey said that they had been involved in traffic accidents or violations while under the influence of cocaine.

A glance at Appendix B demonstrates how illogical cocaine-related state laws are.

The effect of the lack of uniformity for simple possession of small quantities of cocaine, for a first offender, can best be illustrated by a few examples:

• Mr. C. is arrested for driving under the influence. A search reveals that he is in possession of one gram of cocaine.

If arrested in Utah or Wyoming, the greatest penalty he would face is six months in jail. Arrested in Texas or Missouri, he would face up to 20 years in prison.

Let's look at what happens to someone arrested in three states so close to each other that people regularly commute from one to another of them, or drive to restaurants or parties from one state to the other.

• Ms. E. is arrested for speeding. She is a resident of New York State. She is found to have less than one gram of cocaine. In New York, as a first offender, she could be jailed for one year. If she were picked up in Connecticut, she could be jailed for seven years; in New Jersey, for five years.

These major disparities in sentencing are not justified by logic or by the differences in the incidence of cocaine use, so far as one can see. The underlying theories concerning the extent of punishment for simple possession appears to be that the greater the punishment, the greater the deterrence or, put another way, the less likely the occurrence of the crime. The second theory is that simple possession implies that there is no victim other than the person involved. Thus, it is a victimless crime, and it should be punished with a lighter sentence. We have repeatedly shown that the use of cocaine escalates so rapidly among some people that it quickly claims victims other than the abuser. Further, there is ample evidence of a relationship between heavy cocaine use and the commission of serious crimes. The notion that cocaine claims no victims is naive, at best, and fallacious as well as dangerous.

As a glance at column two of Appendix B shows, state laws on the possession of "excessive" quantities of cocaine, make equally little sense. While all are based on the assumption that greater quantities imply trafficking, the definition of what is excessive varies. While some states have decided that 28 grams or one ounce or more demonstrates conclusively that the possessor is also a trafficker, one state, Vermont, requires the possession of only one-half gram to define a trafficker.

Convictions for trafficking usually result in sentences of from 15 years to life imprisonment, and normally preclude suspended sentences and parole. But here, too, there is considerable variation. The lack of uniformity among the states results in further inequity, as shown in the following example:

• Mr. L. is arrested for driving under the influence, and a search reveals 112 grams, or 4 ounces, of cocaine in his possession.

If he is arrested in New York, he faces life imprisonment, with a 15-year mandatory minimum. If in nearby Massachusetts, he could be sentenced to 30 years, with a 5-year mandatory minimum. In Florida, for varying periods up to 30 years with parole possible after three to five years. Arrest in South Dakota would carry a sentence of no more than two years.

States without trafficking laws have other ways of addressing the issue. They may rely upon statutes that permit a jury to make the commonsense inference that someone found with a substantial amount of cocaine is guilty of "possession with unlawful intent." Where such laws are in effect, the penalty is for a jury to decide, and it may or may not be severe enough to be a deterrent to dealing. In any case, the difference in penalties for simple possession and intent to deal suggests that personal consumption of cocaine is viewed as tolerable even by our legal system.

In an effort to protect children from dealers, statutes have been adopted in many states proscribing the sale or delivery of cocaine to anyone younger than 18 years of age. This generally applies to adults dealing to young people. To eliminate the phenomenon of older children providing coke to younger ones, which is quite common, some laws provide penalties applicable to minors dealing coke to youngsters three years younger than themselves. Most laws, however, do not cover the main suppliers of children, that is, other children.

Although the possession, manufacture, sale, and distribution of cocaine are unlawful, the great majority of states do not have statutes making its *use* unlawful, as Appendix B shows. Perhaps the absence of such legislation relates to concerns about invasion of privacy and protection of individual rights. It would seem possible, however, to strike a balance between the competing rights of individuals, on the one hand, and of society, on the other.

It has been argued that the laws pertaining to simple possession by extension also punish use, but that argument seems to me to be extremely limited. Sending a person to jail or levying a fine do nothing about treating what might more usefully be regarded as an illness. Recognizing the problem, 17 states and the Virgin Islands have enacted "second-chance" statutes. Most of these allow courts to defer sentencing of a user found guilty of first-time possession. The user is generally placed on treatment probation for a period not to exceed two years. Upon completion of the probation without untoward incident, the user's case is dismissed and all the criminal records are sealed, or in the case of minors, the records are destroyed. Unfortunately, many of the states do not require periodic blood tests to confirm the user's drug-free status. Without this confirmation, the second-chance statutes may simply succeed in educating the user to be more prudent.

A few states have so-called "nuisance" laws that prosecute people found on the premises of a place where drugs are used, manufactured, or stored.

Perhaps the most pressing need in the area of the law and drugs is the recognition that treatment of drug dependence is as important, if not more important, than punishment. But how to get a drug addict into treatment, when he is more prone to deny that he has a problem than he is to seek help for it, is a dilemma. Involuntary commitment for treatment is subject to serious abuse, which is why many states have opted out of dealing with the issue. However, there is precedent for such commitment: Physicians along with family members in all states already have the authority to recommend the commitment of seriously depressed, suicidal, or psychotic patients to prevent imminent harm to themselves or others.

Two states have thus far taken action on the compulsory drug treatment issue. In Connecticut, a relative or a police official who believes that a person is drug dependent (on narcotics or cocaine) may petition a court for compulsory treatment. The court may order commitment to an inpatient facility with a drug treatment program for a period of from 90 days to two years. The person may be released in less than 90 days if it is shown that he or she has responded to treatment.

Similarly, a new Texas statute that became effective in August 1983, permits court-ordered commitment to a mental hospital of a drug-dependent person upon the request of a county official, a district attorney, or any adult who has reason to believe that the person may do harm to himself or to others. Two physicians must attest that the person in question is drug-dependent and should be committed.

Both the Connecticut and Texas laws provide legal protection for the person to be committed, including documentation of the condition for which he is to be treated, representation by an attorney of his choice, and opportunity to contest the commitment.

It seems to me that concerned citizens working with local bar associations could press for laws specifically addressed to cocaine use. Such statutes should declare unequivocally that use of the drug is unlawful and will be punished with increasingly stiff sentences starting with first offenders. Appropriate mandatory treatment should be a key requirement along with supervised probation for varying periods of time. One requirement during the probationary period should be blood or urine tests to monitor for traces of the drug.

Other laws with teeth in them should deal with the issue of driving while drug impaired. In addition to mandatory drug detection tests, such laws should set increasingly severe limits on driving—up to and including restrictions on driving or suspension of a license for periods of a year or more. Some jobs should require drug-free status as a condition of employment. Further, blood/urine tests should be mandatory. Both these elements should be part of the job description. For the public good, bus drivers, train motormen, secret service officers, airline mechanics and pilots, school-bus drivers, nuclear power reactor personnel, and cab drivers, among others, should be included. That such a program works is demonstrated by the experience of the Navy. When it instituted a mandatory testing program, drug use dropped from about 50 percent in 1980 to 5 percent in 1983. The visually impaired are kept away from the driver's seat without complaint that their civil rights have been denied; why not the drug impaired? The public deserves this protection. Violators of this trust should be dealt with swiftly, being required to undergo treatment and to remain under surveillance until it is established that their drug dependence is under control.

Accessories to cocaine use should know that they, too, risk serious trouble under the law if they aid or abet its use in any way. Thus, permitting a guest to bring cocaine into one's home or car, or allowing its use on these premises, should be perceived as breaking the law with serious consequences for the "innocent" party.

Finally, the move now under way among seven Northeastern states to set a uniform minimum drinking age to help reduce highway accidents and deaths might serve as a model for uniform regional laws applying to illicit drug use. This can surely be done while preserving states rights and local autonomy.

The helping professions—physicians, psychologists, and social workers—also can contribute substantially to the drive to reduce and eliminate drug dependency. But first they must educate themselves about the nature of the problem. At the present time, few medical schools or schools of social work require courses in the nature, consequences, and treatment of drug abuse. Many psychiatrists and psychologists still believe, in the face of mounting evidence to the contrary, that drug dependence is a symptom of a deeply rooted neurosis that must be treated first if the symptom, drug dependence, is to be eliminated. Drug addiction specialists, I among them, simply do not believe this to be the case for the great majority of drug-dependent people. We believe, based on our experience, that drug addiction can be and should be treated as a discrete illness, by programs of detoxification combined with group and individual therapy to help the afflicted person gain insight into his problem which is addiction.

In recognition of the gaps in physician knowledge about drug addiction, I believe that medical schools should begin adding appropriate courses to their curricula. I also strongly believe that regional seminars of various kinds are essential to provide physician education on a continuing basis.

In addition, physicians can take some simple practical steps that could prove helpful to their patients. As part of their continuing care of children, pediatricians with the consent of parents, should not only educate their young patients about drugs, but should also, at the appropriate time, include drug and alcohol testing, for example, as part of their usual checkup protocol. When they keep in mind that drug experimentation begins early in this country, by age 12 among many youngsters, they will feel more comfortable about such an approach. Early detection can save lives and reduce the need for inpatient treatment. Waiting until the child is so sick that the diagnosis is made when the physician says hello to the child is cruel and, unnecessary, and too late in many cases.

They should examine their own drug-prescribing practices as a first step in cutting drug abuse and misuse. Mood-altering drugs, including sleeping pills, tranquilizers, and stimulants, avoid and postpone dealing with the stress of daily living and help set the stage for the acceptance of drugs as a way of life. Cocaine thus becomes just another way of avoiding reality, of trying to live the pleasure principle. Physicians should operate on the principle that has for millennia guided medical practice: Doctor, Do No Harm.

In the area of public policy, the federal government appears to be ambivalent about the American drug problem. While on the one hand there is constant reference to the seriousness of drug abuse, and the First Lady participates in parents conferences and other events exploring the issue, federal funds for drug enforcement activities and for research either are cut sharply or fail to keep pace with inflation. At the present time, despite the best efforts of various police agencies, we capture only about 10 percent of the illicit drugs crossing our borders. The budget of the National Institute of Drug Abuse has been cut when drug-related research is desperately needed.

The problem of cocaine abuse is undoubtedly growing more urgent. We learned from 800–Cocaine that the major constraint on cocaine use is its price. We know that coca cultivation and processing are expanding and that more cocaine is entering the U.S. market daily. With cocaine, as with any other product, the more of it there is, the lower the price. It is an ominous sign that the price of the drug is falling, that as we have noted earlier a kilo of cocaine which cost approximately $60,000 a year ago now costs about $30,000. When the governments of Colombia, Bolivia, and Peru profit so mightly from the coke business, why should they cut production? Especially in the face of escalating demand by the American people.

In the long run, it is up to each of us to decide how we feel about cocaine. The media is trying to help with negative cocaine articles, movies and TV shows but the presence and longevity of 800–Cocaine says it all—cocaine is not chic; it is a drug thats dangerous and addicting. The drug lords will be put out of business only if we decide that we will not be customers, will not pay for our own destruction. We have to believe that there is no such thing as recreational use of cocaine. We have to reach both adults and children or we will win one battle and lose the war. We now know that within a short time of initiating use of the drug, many of us will become addicted and will thus acquire a lifelong, chronic, relapsing illness. When a disease has no known cause, and no known pathology, and no definitive treatment, prevention is the only avenue for hope. We have it in our power to beat back the epidemic. It's up to us.

Appendix A
800-Cocaine Research Questionnaire

DEMOGRAPHICS

Age	_____	Route	_____
Sex	_____	Amount	_____
City	_____	Race	_____
State	_____	Education	_____ (yrs)
Employed	_____ (y/n)	Cocaine Duration	_____
Job	_____	Income	_____ 0–10,000
			_____ 10,000–25,000
			_____ 25,000–50,000
			_____ 50,000

COCAINE HISTORY

Started at age _____
Started with _____ route
Present route _____
Spent $_____ last week on cocaine
Do you use: (Choose one)

_____ daily _____ More than once/week
_____ weekly _____ Whenever it is available
_____ less than once/month

What was the most cocaine you yourself used in a day:
_____ (gm) _____ (dollars)
Is cocaine your favorite drug: _____ (yes)
_____ (no)
If no, what is: _____

74

What is the major factor limiting your cocaine use:

_____ cost   _____ religion

_____ discipline   _____ other (specify)

Have you ever used cocaine almost continuously until your supply was exhausted:

_____ yes

_____ no

Have you ever used heroin or other narcotics: _____

You called 800–COCAINE

1. _____ for information
2. _____ for help
3. _____ to help someone else
4. _____ to check it out
5. _____ other (specify)

<u>COCAINE DEPENDENCE</u> (Check as many as apply)
(Coke-A-Holic)

I. Group 1 NEGATIVE MEDICAL EFFECTS

1. _____ physical deterioration
2. _____ general health failure
3. _____ loss of energy
4. _____ insomnia
5. _____ sore throat
6. _____ nose bleeds
7. _____ need for plastic or nasal repair surgery
8. _____ headaches
9. _____ voice problems
10. _____ sinus problems
11. _____ running nose
12. _____ lost sex drive
13. _____ poor or decreased sexual performance
14. _____ trembling
15. _____ seizures or convulsions
16. _____ nausea or vomiting
17. _____ can't stop licking lips or grinding teeth
18. _____ constant sniffing or rubbing nose
19. _____ loss of consciousness
20. _____ trouble breathing or swallowing
21. _____ heart palpitations (flutters)
22. _____ decreased interest in personal health or hygiene (e.g., last MD/DDS appointment)
23. _____ other (specify)

How severe do you think are these problems:

_____ mild   _____ no real problem

_____ severe   _____ moderate

Has a physical problem caused you to stop using:

_____ yes   _____ no

If yes, for how long: _____ days

II. Group 2 NEGATIVE PSYCHIATRIC EFFECTS

   1. _____ jitteryness
   2. _____ anxiety
   3. _____ depression
   4. _____ panic
   5. _____ fears
   6. _____ irritability
   7. _____ delusions (false beliefs)
   8. _____ suspiciousness
   9. _____ paranoia
  10. _____ concentration problems
  11. _____ hearing voices in head
  12. _____ other hallucinations
  13. _____ loss of interest in friends
  14. _____ loss of interest in nondrug-related activities
  15. _____ memory problems
  16. _____ thoughts of suicide
  17. _____ attempted suicide
  18. _____ blackouts
  19. _____ compulsive behaviors (e.g., combing hair, straightening tie, tapping feet, or others)
  20. _____ must take other drugs or alcohol to calm down
  21. _____ decreased interest in appearance
  22. _____ other (specify)

III. DEPENDENCE

   1. _____ think you are addicted
   2. _____ real need for cocaine
   3. _____ significant distress without cocaine
   4. _____ can't turn it down when it is available
   5. _____ unable to stop using for one month
   6. _____ trying to force self to limit use
   7. _____ binge use (24 hours or more of near continuous use)
   8. _____ use of cocaine resulting in missing work or rescheduling an appointment or breaking a date or family/social obligation

9. _____ prefer cocaine to talking to friends
10. _____ prefer cocaine to family activities
11. _____ prefer cocaine to sex
12. _____ prefer cocaine to food
13. _____ use cocaine in A.M. before breakfast
14. _____ use of cocaine has led to the need for excuses
15. _____ reduced focus on work and promotion
16. _____ borrowing from friends and family
17. _____ dealing
18. _____ other illicit activity to support habit
19. _____ fear of being discovered as a user
20. _____ usually use cocaine alone
21. _____ Monday absenteeism
22. _____ loss of control over cocaine
23. _____ if you stop using, you get depressed or crash or
lose energy or motivation

IV. SOCIAL AND OTHER PROBLEMS
1. _____ arrests because of the drug
2. _____ unusual behavior for you while intoxicated
3. _____ job/career problems
4. _____ loss of job
5. _____ loss of spouse or loved one(s)
6. _____ traffic violations due to cocaine
7. _____ traffic accidents due to cocaine
8. _____ loss of friends
9. _____ fighting or arguments due to cocaine
10. _____ impaired coordination or injuries due to cocaine
11. _____ court case pending
12. _____ loss of pre-cocaine values
13. _____ threats of separation or divorce
14. _____ threats of being thrown out of the house

V. ADVERSE OPINIONS
1. _____ people keep telling me I'm different
2. _____ wife/husband/lover objects to use
3. _____ wife/husband/lover objects to amount
4. _____ other important people object
5. _____ feel guilty about effect I'm having on others

VI. FINANCES (As a result of cocaine)
1. _____ in debt
2. _____ no money left
3. _____ used 50% or more of savings

4. _____ caused me to steal or borrow without repaying
5. _____ stole from work
6. _____ stole from family or friends

Why do you continue to use:
_____ for the high
_____ to prevent a crash
_____ for confidence or energy
_____ for sexual arousal
_____ for relief of boredom
_____ for relief of fatigue or lack of energy

Is your cocaine use a threat to:
_____ your psychological health
_____ physical health
_____ relationships
_____ career
_____ happiness

Do you think you ever had withdrawal symptoms when you stopped using:
_____ yes   _____ no

So far in your life how much have you spent on cocaine
$_____

If you had $100 to spend on leisure activities (recreation) would you spend it on (Check one):
_____ theater-records-movie-video cassettes
_____ cocaine
_____ going out with friends
_____ going out with family

Appendix B
Penalties: State by State

Penalties for first offenders* found in possession of small quantities of cocaine†; minimum amounts presumed to imply intent to traffic‡; and states with and without statutes pertaining to use.

State	Possession 1st Off. Penalty (years)	Trafficking Minimum Am't. (grams)	Use statutes Yes	No
Alabama	2–15	28		no
Alaska	0–5	—		no
Arizona	2–5	—	yes (6 mos)	
Arkansas	0–1 (< 2 gms)	2		no
California	2–10	—		no
Colorado	4–8	—	yes (2 yrs)	
Connecticut	0–7	28		no
Delaware	0–5	15	yes (5 yrs)	
District of Columbia	0–1		yes (1 yr)	
Florida	0–5	28		no
Georgia	2–15	28		no
Hawaii	5	3.5		no
Idaho	0–3	—		no

State	Possession 1st Off. Penalty (years)	Trafficking Minimum Am't. (grams)	Use statutes Yes	No
Illinois	1–3	30		no
Indiana	1–4	3		no
Iowa	0–1	—		no
Kansas	3–5 (Min) 10–15 (Max)	—		no
Kentucky	1–5	no minimum specified		no
Louisiana	0–5	28		no
Maine	1–3	no minimum specified		no
Maryland	0–4	28		no
Massachusetts	0–1	28		no
Michigan	0–4	50		no
Minnesota	0–5	—		no
Mississippi	0–3	—		no
Missouri	0–20 if prison 6 mos–1 yr if county jail	—		no
Montana	0–5	—		no
Nebraska	0–5	20		no
Nevada	1–6	—	yes (1 yr)	
New Hampshire	0–7	—		no
New Jersey	0–5	28 (containing 3.5 gms pure)	yes	
New Mexico	0–1 1–5	—	yes (1 yr)	
New York	0–1	3.5		no
North Carolina	0–2	28		no
North Dakota	0–5	—		no
Ohio	18 mos–5 yrs	30 gms or 75 doses	yes (5 yrs)	
Oklahoma	2–10	—		no
Oregon	0–5	—		no
Pennsylvania	0–1	—		no
Rhode Island	0–3	—		no
South Carolina	0–2 (if < 10 grains)	10		no

State	Possession 1st Off. Penalty (years)	Trafficking Minimum Am't. (grams)	Use statutes Yes No	
South Dakota	0–2	—		no
Tennessee	0–11 mos 29 days	—		no
Texas	2–20	28		no
Utah	0–6 mos	—		no
Vermont	0–1	500 mgms		no
Virginia	1–10 years	—		no
Washington	0–5	—		no
West Virginia	90 days– 6 mos	—		no
Wisconsin	0–1	—		no
Wyoming	0–6	—	yes (90 days)	

*For subsequent offenses, penalties are often doubled.
†Usually, less than ½ gram.
‡Conviction for trafficking is a felony with mandatory punishment. A judge has no discretion but to sentence for a specific period without the possibility of parole. The duration of the sentence relates to the quantity found on the person. For example, in Florida, the possession of 28–200 grams brings a mandatory minimum sentence of three years without parole, but a judge could sentence up to 30 years with a provision for parole after three years. There is also a fine of $50,000. Possession of 200–400 grams brings a mandatory sentence of 5 years without parole, with a maximum sentence up to 30 years with parole to begin after 5 years. The fine is $100,000. For possession of 400 grams or more, the mandatory minimum sentence is 15 years; the fine is $250,000.

Note: This table is for reference only and is not definitive. While the data come from official sources, amendment and changes are frequent.

Appendix C
A Non-User's Guide to Cocaine Paraphernalia

Any of this paraphernalia can be purchased in retail stores, some of it as jewelry.

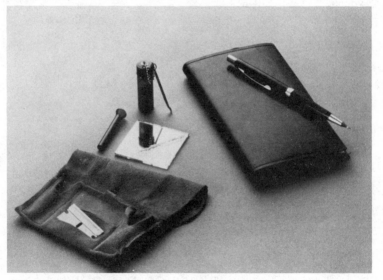

The "executive" kit.

Inconspicuous in a pocket, purse, or briefcase, this small kit contains everything a cocaine abuser needs: a mirror (smooth surface), a spoon for snorting, a razor for chopping and a glass "tooter" for snorting, too. In a matter of minutes cocaine can be abused in the washroom or behind an office door.

The freebase kit.

Freebasing is becoming the most popular and addicting form of abuse. "Street cocaine," or cocaine hydrochloride is mixed with ammonium hydroxide ether in a beaker or petri dish. This pasty substance is heated to evaporate the ether, leaving unadulterated cocaine freebase.

Small amounts, or "hits," are placed on the screens in the neck of the pipe and smoked at high temperature over the torch. This creates a "rush" as intense as injecting cocaine, but without the needle.

The ether, of course, is extremely volatile and may explode. These freebase components are readily available in the retail marketplace.

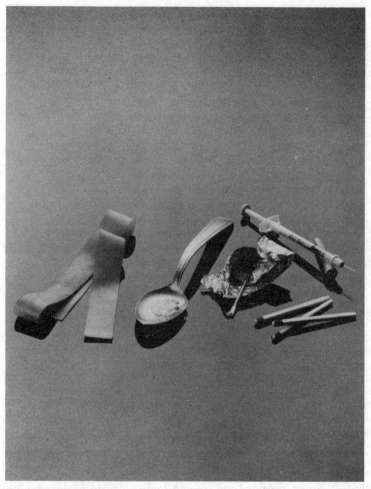

Intravenous use.

As much as a gram of cocaine hydrochloride, or street cocaine, can be dissolved in water and drawn into a syringe. A vein is tied off with the tourniquet, or "tie," and the cocaine solution injected directly into the vein.

The onset of the cocaine effect, or "rush" is immediate, and lasts up to ten minutes. The total effect may last 30 minutes. The cocaine can be heated briefly, but it is not necessary.

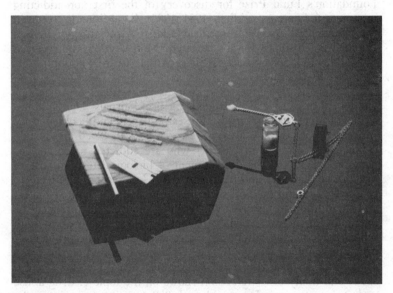

Intranasal use.

Cocaine, spilled on a hard, flat surface, is chopped into "lines" with the razor to make it more powdery.

Lines may vary in the amount of cocaine, depending on the user's habits.

It is "snorted" intranasally and absorbed into the mucous membranes of the nasal cavity.

Cocaine may be snorted from a small "coke spoon," or up a "tooter," a short glass or metal tube, cut-off straws or rolled up paper money, as depicted in movies and on television.

The rush is less intense, the onset slower due to the slower absorption; the effect lasting 15 to 30 minutes.

About the Author

Mark S. Gold, M.D., is director of research at both Fair Oaks Hospital, in Summit, New Jersey, and the Regent Hospital, in New York City. Dr. Gold is the founder and medical director of the National Cocaine Helpline. Dr. Gold received his doctor of medicine from the University of Florida College of Medicine in Gainesville, Florida. Dr. Gold was a neurobehavioral fellow, resident, chief resident and faculty member in the department of psychiatry at the Yale University School of Medicine. A Phi Beta Kappa, Dr. Gold was awarded the annual American Psychiatric Foundation's Fund Prize for discovery of the first non-addicting treatment for narcotic addicts (1981–1982). In addition he received the Presidential Award from the National Association of Private Psychiatric Hospitals for his research. More recently he received the Public Relations Society's Silver Anvil Award for public service for 800–Cocaine.

Dr. Gold is a member of numerous professional organizations and an editor of several prestigious medical journals. Dr. Gold has authored more than 400 medical research papers and books, mostly concerned with the two areas of research he is involved in: identification and treatment of patients who are addicted to cocaine or narcotic drugs, and the development of biological tests for use in psychiatric diagnosis and treatment. Dr. Gold teaches and lectures at universities and medical societies throughout the United States, and in addition to his research, teaching, and clinical practice, he maintains an active schedule of public service lectures to high school students and parent groups concerned with the problem of drug abuse among our youth. Dr. Gold has appeared on the *Today Show*, *Good Morning America*, *CBS Morning News*, *The Phil Donahue Show*, and many other television shows on the topic of drug abuse and its prevention. Dr. Gold and 800–Cocaine have been the subject of ABC, NBC, CNN, and CBS network news coverage and articles by the United Press International, Associated Press, *Time* magazine, *Newsweek*, *Reader's Digest*, *The Wall Street Journal* and *The New York Times*.

Dr. Gold was married in 1971 to Janice Robin Finn, his high school sweetheart, and they have three children, a dog, and a beach house on Hutchinson Island, Florida.